ANDRÉ GIDE

DOSTOEVSKY

Introductory Note to the First English Edition, 1925,
by ARNOLD BENNETT

New Introduction by ALBERT J. GUERARD

"Dostoevsky was the only psychologist from whom I had
anything to learn: he belongs to the happiest windfalls of
my life, happier even than the discovery of Stendhal."
NIETZSCHE

A NEW DIRECTIONS PAPERBOOK

FIFTH PRINTING

To
M. A. G.

NOTE

IN the early months of 1922, M. André Gide delivered before M. Jacques Copeau's School of Dramatic Art at the *Vieux-Colombier* a series of eight addresses on DOSTOEVSKY, first published from shorthand notes—with but slender emendation, lest the style should lose in spontaneity—in the *Revue Hebdomadaire*, Nos. 2–8, 1923, then later in the same year in book form, together with selected essays. These addresses form the basis of the present volume from which one short chapter, an *Allocution lue au Vieux-Colombier pour la Célébration du Centenaire de Dostoïevsky*, has been omitted because the Author adapted his preface specially for the English edition from it. For the 1961 edition New Directions has reinstated Gide's lecture on *Les Frères Karamazov* with the permission of the copyright owners. It was translated by Louise Varèse.

By courtesy of Messrs. William Heinemann, we are permitted to quote extensively from Mrs. Constance Garnett's translations of *Dostoevsky's Novels* (12 vols., 1912–1920). We have utilized as far as possible Miss Ethel Colburn Mayne's *Letters of Fyodor Michailovitch Dostoevsky to his Family and Friends* (Messrs. Chatto and Windus, 1917): elsewhere we have cited J. W. Bienstock's *Correspondance et Voyage à l'Étranger* (Paris, 1908). Quotations are further made from Bienstock and Nau's version of the *Journal* (Paris, 1904), and from *Th. M. Dostoevsky: eine biographische Studie,* by N. Hoffmann (Berlin, 1899).

CONTENTS

INTRODUCTION

HOW much has changed since 1925, when Arnold Bennett wrote his modest little introductory note to the English edition of André Gide's *Dostoevsky*! It seemed necessary, then, to remark that Gide "writes in the very midst of morals," and even necessary to insist (given the "various and distressing personal defects") on Dostoevsky's humanity and wisdom. More than a third of a century has passed, during which the fortunes of Bennett himself have declined, and those of the massive Edwardian realism he so ably represented. Meanwhile, Gide died in apotheosis, in 1951: the corruptor of youth suitably honored, at the end, by the Ministry of Education. But in 1925 (and all the more in 1922, when the Dostoevsky lectures were given) Gide had not yet achieved his place as the "representative European" and "representative contemporary" . . . the embodied consciousness of an epoch. This was to come with the astonishing paradoxical display of 1926 and 1927. For in those years the same author published a sprightly yet major antirealistic novel (*The Counterfeiters*), a great puritanic confession of homosexuality (in *If It Die . . .*), a diary of religious experience (*Numquid et tu . . .?*) and a compassionate report of brutal capitalist exploitation in the Congo (*Voyage au Congo*). A diabolic comprehensiveness and ethic of oscillation, which left his enemies trembling! And now the general public was simultaneously assaulted by Gide's multiple contradictions.

As for Dostoevsky (and though in 1950 he was still very poorly represented in French public and university libraries) . . . he stands very securely at the summit of the novel, throwing his great dark shadow over the genre. But in 1922 Gide was speaking to an audience of intellectuals who had perhaps read neither *Notes from Underground* nor *The Possessed,* and certainly not *The Eternal Husband.* And thus we see him stress, "point out" almost, certain traits of the Dostoevskyan hero now bruited in undergraduate classes on the novel—the delight in degradation, for example, or the sudden radical shifts in feeling.

The texts to follow are not of equal merit and interest, though all are worth reading. "Dostoevsky in His Correspondence" (1908) is a vivid but rambling evocation of contradictions, and "The Brothers Karamazov" seems little more than a program note. The "Addresses on Dostoevsky" (1922) are themselves uneven in quality, betraying both their origin on the lecture platform and their subsequent dictation to a secretary . . . not to mention the vagaries of translation. Even in its present form, the first lecture reveals the unprofessional speaker's lack of confidence, his fear (duly noted in the *Journal*) that he might run out of things to say. Hence the dependence on very ample quotation. But by the fourth lecture Gide had mastered the highly subjective approach and evocative voice which was to give this work its great and suspect charm. The lectures become intensely personal, as the best work of Gide regularly does; this engaging troubling voice seems to come from within ourselves. Gide speaks more generously of Dostoevsky than most writers are wont to speak of other writers, and almost apologizes for noting a flaw: the impulse to "prove." His enthusiasm is infectious and unquestionably sincere. But it is also evident that Gide finds the Dostoevsky he seeks; that, quite admittedly, he here presents his "own ethic under cover of Dostoevsky's."

". . . I am eager to get back to my novel. But everything I find means of saying through Dostoevsky and apropos of him is dear to me and I attach a great importance to it. It will be, just as much as a book of criticism, a book of confessions, to anyone who knows how to read; or rather: a profession of faith." Thus Gide wrote in his *Journal* for April 22, 1922. The portrait of Dostoevsky is another Gidean self-portrait, though not a portrait of the artist. Gide was an important theorist on the art of fiction, but he has almost nothing to say about Dostoevsky's technique, except in one fine paragraph in the third lecture. There he speaks of the impulse to create "as many cross-connections as possible," and of Dostoevsky's use of shadow:

> In one of Stendhal's novels, the light is constant, steady, and well-diffused. Every object is lit up in the same way, and is visible equally well from all angles; there are no shadow effects. But in Dostoevsky's books, as in a Rembrandt portrait, the shadows are the essential. Dostoevsky groups his characters and happenings, plays a brilliant light upon them, illuminating one aspect only. Each of his characters has a deep setting of shadow, reposes on its own shadow almost.

These were notably Gide's own concerns in *The Counterfeiters,* which was then under way: to make many cross-connections, and to create such a shadowed personage as Strouvilhou. In novel-writing as elsewhere Gide puritanically gave in to the most uncongenial of temptations. The rational, limited Gide envied Dostoevsky's "*inconséquences,*" as he must have envied his abundant creativity, his archaic roughness and possessed energy. But these he would never achieve. From early in his career and to the last days of his life Gide admonished himself to write in a less measured and orderly way, and to overcome the neat patternings of French realism and the *roman d'analyse.*

It is nevertheless not Dostoevsky the artist that concerned Gide, but Dostoevsky the turbulent moralist: the psychologist, philosopher and Christian. "In my eyes [the] ideas are all that is most precious in Dostoevsky and I have made them my own." The act of assimilation is a loving one. Characteristically, Gide hardly speaks of the ideas and attitudes that would repel or leave him indifferent: the political conservativism, for instance. What mattered to Gide was the Dostoevsky he could *use*. Quite as characteristically he put his subject beside others in a personal Pantheon, the others too standing in a selective and purified form: Browning and Blake, Nietzsche and Baudelaire. Strange companions they might seem, to many historians of ideas! Yet Gide saw all five as theorists of the divided ego and menaced consciousness. All five, he believed, argued the value of discord and discontinuity, and preached freedom won through self-destruction. These were cornerstones of his own thought (as well as sources of personal anxiety); inevitably he had to find them in his masters, or choose masters who seemed to possess them.

Three things stand out, three philosophical fantasies or fictions which contain their human truth.

First, the theory of the divided ego and of an absolute ambivalence. The crucial passage appears near the end of the fourth lecture, where Gide speaks of the dualities of Dostoevskyan characters:

They have no connection, or at least but little, with the frequently observed pathological states, where a second personality is grafted upon the original, the one alternating with the other . . . so that ere long we have two distinct personalities sharing the one fleshly tenement. They change places, the one succeeding the other in turn, all the time ignorant of its neighbour. . . . But in Dostoevsky the most disconcerting feature is the simultaneity of such phenomena, and the fact that each character never relinquishes consciousness of his dual personality with its inconsistencies.

The theory of simultaneity[1] is a pleasing philosophical fiction, comparable to that of the gratuitous act; it is amusing to think of tension and anxiety so total. But if Gide's words apply well enough to the narrator of *Notes from Underground,* they do not apply to Golyadkin of *The Double,* descending into psychosis, nor do they apply to many others suffering from mildly neurotic disruptions. It is strange to observe Gide avoid all Freudian categories in speaking of these dark matters. It is also strange to find him saying so little about the *external* doubles who appear so often in Dostoevsky's novels: those primitive or accusing figures who actually seem to embody fragments of the subject's personality. Thus Pyotr may be Stavrogin's "shadow," as Gide observes. But it is the convict Fedka who enacts his suppressed desires. He too is a double, and of a kind overlooked by Gide.

The Possessed also served Gide's ethical theory of affirmation through renunciation, and his fiction or intuition of eternal life to be entered into here and now. "For whoever will save his life shall lose it; but whosoever will lose his life for My sake, the same shall save it." This is the sacred text to which, over many decades, Gide succeeded in attaching the most diverse and even diabolic meanings. In *Dostoevsky,* however,

[1] Gide's theory of (or, wish for) simultaneity and ambivalence is expressed most clearly in his preface to the *Fleurs du Mal*: "That there is—against this cohesive force keeping the individual consistent with himself, and by which (as Spinoza said) he tends 'to persist in his own being'—another force, centrifugal and disaggregative, by which the individual tends to divide himself, to strive for dissociation, to risk himself, to gamble himself and to lose himself. . . . I won't go so far as to say that Baudelaire anticipated this as clearly as, for instance, Dostoevsky. But I cannot read without a shudder of recognition and terror these few sentences from his intimate diary: *The taste for productive concentration should replace, in a mature man, the taste for loss of self*—or, further, *there are in every man at every hour two appeals which are* SIMULTANEOUS (the entire interest of the sentence is in this word): *one toward God, the other toward Satan.*" *Oeuvres complètes,* VII, 503–4. My translation.

he makes his valuable distinction between the humiliation that "damns" and the humility that "sanctifies." The reward of true renunciation of personality is immediate enjoyment of eternal life. What does Gide "really mean" by this? He seems uncertain, as was Dostoevsky himself, whether to take Kirilov as madman or as lucid existential saint. And he uneasily balances the eternity of scriptural *joy* with the blissful eternity of the epileptic, said to endure five seconds. These subtleties are bemusing and attractive. More simply and more humbly, Gide emphasizes Dostoevsky's repudiation of intellect and pride. The meek shall inherit the earth.

The strange figure of Kirilov fascinated Gide as early as 1899, in the *Lettres à Angèle*. He returns to him again and again in these lectures, as Albert Camus would return to him in *Le Mythe de Sisyphe*. Gide too wanted to write his Life of a Great Sinner, and he too wanted to dramatize the Devil. Curiously enough, the mild Kirilov becomes the model for the seducer Vincent of *The Counterfeiters*; Vincent proves himself to be the Devil by the same logic Kirilov used to prove himself God. The absurd and philosophical suicide of Kirilov, moreover, served as pretext for more than one meditation on the gratuitous act. Even the whimsical youthful Lafcadio may be in Kirilov's debt. By 1922 Gide had retreated from the extremes of his theory of gratuity, and could refer less perversely to an "absence of outward motivation." That is comprehensible enough. Yet Gide would be attracted to the end of his life by the conviction or illusion that true breaks in the streams of personality and consciousness could occur and could be richly creative. The Nietzschean "strong man" (to be both cherished and feared) found new energy through fission of the self, through destruction of inward order. And so too the individualists of Dostoevsky and Gide.

All this is but to reiterate that *Dostoevsky* is as much a revelation of its creator as of its subject. It is surely one of the most unacademic critiques ever written. Would it not be even more exact to call it a very protestant book in method and in spirit: *Six Sermons on Dostoevsky?* The tendentious selection and subtle grouping of quotations to serve as pretexts for moral utterance, the rhythmical return to certain key passages, the personal suasion of a living audience through a highly vocal style, the incorrigible love of paradox, the alternations of difficult reasonings and reassuring personal anecdote (the Walter Rathenau meeting), the building at last to a climax of ethical eloquence—surely these typical maneuverings of the protestant pastor could hardly be better exemplified than by the last pages of the fifth "Address."

Gide on Dostoevsky, then; but also Dostoevsky on Gide. A great deal of the Russian novelist is missing from these pages. There is little in these lectures about the complications of the great long novels, nor about the power and diversity of Dostoevsky's creation. Therefore no reader should be content with this one book, nor take any of its dicta on faith. Yet if one could keep only one book on Dostoevsky, I would be tempted to keep this one. It conveys as few critical books I know the excitement of intensely personal and sympathetic reading, and the shock of recognition. At least it starts, however irresponsibly, many important questionings. So at least it has been for me. It was Gide's little book, rather than any more balanced academic study, that sent me back to Dostoevsky some years ago, prepared to enjoy his work more intensely than before.

ALBERT J. GUERARD

1961

INTRODUCTORY NOTE TO THE FIRST
ENGLISH EDITION OF 1925

ANDRÉ GIDE is now one of the leaders of French
Literature. The first book of his to attract wide attention among the lettered was *L'Immoraliste*. Since then, in
some twenty years of productiveness, he has gradually con-
solidated his position until at the present day his admirers
are entitled to say that no other living French author stands
so firm and so passionately acknowledged as an influence.
His authority over the schools of young writers who contribute to or are published by *La Nouvelle Revue Française*
(with which he has been intimately connected from its
foundation) is quite unrivalled. And it must be stated, as a
final proof of mastership, that he has powerful and not
despicable opponents.

To my mind his outstanding characteristic is that he is
equally interested in the æsthetic and in the moral aspect of
literature. Few imaginative writers have his broad and
vivacious curiosity about moral problems, and scarcely any
moralists exhibit even half his preoccupation with the
æsthetic. He is a distinguished, if somewhat fragmentary,
literary critic—not merely of French but of Russian, English
and classical literatures. I shall not forget his excitement
when he first read *Tom Jones*. "Ce livre m'attendait," said he,
with grave delight. His practical interest in the technique of
fiction never fades; indeed it grows. So much so that his
latest novel, now appearing serially in *La Nouvelle Revue
Française*, really amounts to an essay in a new form; and with
startling modesty he has labelled it, in the dedication, "my
first novel."

Of course no novelist can achieve anything permanent

without a moral basis or background. Balzac had it; de Maupassant had it to the point of savagery; Zola had it, in his degree. Paul Bourget—a writer whom highbrows French and English have still to reckon with—has it. But André Gide writes in the very midst of morals. They are not only his background, but frequently his foreground. Scarcely one of his books (the exception may be *Les Caves du Vatican*) but poses and attempts to resolve a moral problem.

It was natural and even necessary that such a writer as Gide should deal with such a writer as Dostoevsky. They were made for each other—or rather Dostoevsky was made for Gide. I first met Gide in the immense field of Dostoevsky. He said, and I agreed, that *The Brothers Karamazov* was the greatest novel ever written. This was ages ago, and years have only confirmed us in the opinion.

"But," said Gide, "everything that Dostoevsky ever wrote is worth reading and must be read. Nothing can safely be omitted."

At that period there was none but a mutilated French translation of *The Brothers Karamazov*, and Gide had to read Dostoevsky in German. A complete translation, I fear, still lacks in French, but André Gide can now read him in full in English: which is to our credit and his. Let us, however, not be too much uplifted. Dostoevsky's important *Journal d'un Écrivain* exists in French but not in English.

Those who read Gide's *Dostoevsky* will receive light, some of it dazzling, on both Dostoevsky and Gide. I can recall no other critical work which more cogently justifies and more securely establishes its subject. If anyone wants to appreciate the progress made by Western Europe in the appreciation of Russian psychology, let him compare the late Count Melchior de Vogüé's *Le Roman Russe* with the present work. It is impossible to read this *Dostoevsky* without enlarging one's idea of Dostoevsky and of the functions of the novel. All the conventional charges against the greatest of the Russians—morbidity, etc., etc., fall to pieces during perusal. They are not killed; they merely expire. And Dostoevsky in the end stands out not simply as a supreme psychologist and narrator, but also as a publicist of genius endowed with a prophetic view over the future of the nations as astounding as his insight into the individual. "There never was," says Gide, "an author more Russian in the strictest sense of the word and withal so universally European."

Dostoevsky had various and distressing personal defects, but his humanity and his wisdom, doubtless derived from the man Jesus who delivered the Sermon on the Mount, are unique; and André Gide's demonstration of their worth is his invaluable contribution to Dostoevsky literature.

ARNOLD BENNETT
(1925)

AUTHOR'S PREFACE

TOLSTOY in his immensity still overshadows our horizon; but as a traveller in a land of mountains sees, with each receding step, appear above the nearest peak one loftier yet, screened hitherto by the surrounding heights, some eager spirits herald perchance the rise of Dostoevsky behind Tolstoy's giant figure. This cloud-capped summit is the secret heart of the chain and source of many a generous stream in whose waters the Europe of to-day may slake her strange new thirsts. Dostoevsky, not Tolstoy, merits rank beside Ibsen and Nietzsche: great as they, mayhap the mightiest of the three.

In Germany translations of Dostoevsky are multiplying, each an advance on its predecessor as regards vigour and scrupulous accuracy. England, stubborn and slow to move, yet makes it her concern not to be outstripped. When he introduced Mrs. Constance Garnett's translation in the *New Age*, Arnold Bennett wished all English novelists and short story writers could come under the influence of these "most powerful works of the imagination ever produced." Speaking more particularly of *The Brothers Karamazov*, he declared this book, in which human passion reaches its maximum intensity, contains about a dozen figures that are simply colossal. Who can tell if these colossal figures have ever made, even in Russia, so direct appeal as to us, whether their call sounded ever before so pressing?

Dostoevsky's admirers were recently rare enough, but as invariably happens when the earliest enthusiasts are recruited from the élite, their number goes on increasing steadily. First of all, I should like to inquire how it is that certain minds are still obdurately prejudiced against his work, admirable though it be. Because the best way to overcome a lack of comprehension is to accept it as sincere and try to understand it.

The principal charge brought against Dostoevsky in the name of our Western-European logic has been, I think, the irrational, irresolute, and often irresponsible nature of his characters, everything in their appearance that could seem grotesque and wild. It is not, so people aver, real life that he unfolds, but nightmares. In my belief this is utterly mistaken; but let us grant the truth of it for argument's sake, and refrain from answering after the manner of Freud that there is more sincerity in our dream-life than in the actions of our real existence. Hear rather what Dostoevsky has to say for himself on the subject of dreams: "These obvious absurdities and impossibilities with which your dream was overflowing . . . you accepted all at once, almost without the slightest surprise, at the very time when, on another side, your reason was at its highest tension and showed extraordinary power, cunning, sagacity, and logic. And why, too, on waking and fully returning to reality, do you feel almost every time, and sometimes with extraordinary intensity, that you have left something unexplained behind with the dream, and at the same time you feel that interwoven with these absurdities some thought lies hidden, and a thought that is real, something belonging to your actual life, something that exists and always has existed in your heart. It's as though something new, prophetic, that you were awaiting, has been told you in your dream."[1]

What Dostoevsky says here about dreams we shall apply to his own books, not for a moment that I would consider assimilating these stories to the absurdities of certain dreams, because we feel when we leave one of his books, even should

[1] *The Idiot*, p. 455.

our reason refuse complete agreement with it, that he has laid his finger on some obscure spot "which is part of our actual life." In this, I think, we shall find explained the refusal of certain minds, in the name of Western-European civilization, to admit Dostoevsky's genius, because I readily observe that in all our Western literature (and I do not limit myself to French alone) the novel, with but rare exceptions, concerns itself solely with relations between man and man, passion and intellect, with family, social, and class relations, but never, practically never with the relations between the individual and his self or his God, which are to Dostoevsky all important. I fancy nothing could better illustrate my idea than the reflection made by a Russian and quoted in Mme Hoffmann's biography, the best by far I know, but which unfortunately has not been translated. His reflection, she holds, will enable us to discern one of the peculiarities of the Russian soul. Once reproached with his unpunctuality this Russian gravely retorted: "Yes, life is difficult! There are moments that must be lived well, and this is more important than the keeping of any engagement."[1] The inner life is thus more highly prized than relations with one's fellow-man. Here lies Dostoevsky's secret, the thing which makes him for some so great, for many others so insufferable!

Not for a moment do I suggest that in Western Europe, in France, for example, man is wholly a social being, ever dressed for a part. We have Pascal's *Pensées*, and the *Fleurs du Mal*, strangely solitary and profound, yet as French as any other works in our literature. But a certain category of problems, heart-searchings, passions, and associations seem to be the province of the moralist and the theologian, and a novelist has no call to burden himself with them. The

[1] Hoffmann, p. 7, "Es gibt Augenblicke, die richtig gelebt sein wollen." (*Translator's note.*)

miracle Dostoevsky accomplished consists in this: each of his characters—and he created a world of them—lives by virtue of his own personality, and these intimately personal beings, each with his peculiar secret, are introduced to us in all their puzzling complexity. The wonder of it is that the problems are lived over by each of his characters, or rather let us say the problems exist at the expense of his characters: problems which conflict, struggle, and assume human guise or triumph before our eyes.

No question too transcendent for Dostoevsky to handle in one of his novels; but, having said this, I am bound at once to add that he never approaches a question from the abstract, ideas never exist for him but as functions of his characters, wherein lies their perpetual relativity and source of power. One individual evolves a certain theory concerning God, providence, and life eternal because he knows he must die in a few days' time, in a few hours maybe (Ippolit in *The Idiot*): another (in *The Possessed*) builds up an entire system of metaphysics, containing Nietzsche in embryo, on the premise of self-destruction, for in a quarter of an hour he is going to take his own life, and hearing him speak, it is impossible to distinguish whether his philosophy postulates his suicide or his suicide his philosophy. Prince Myshkim owes his most wonderful, most heavenly raptures to the imminence of an epileptic fit. In conclusion I have only one comment to offer: though pregnant with thought, Dostoevsky's novels are never abstract, indeed, of all the books I know, they are the most palpitating with life.

Representative as Dostoevsky's characters are, they never seem to forsake their humanity to become mere symbols or the types familiar in our classical drama. They keep their individuality which is as specific as in Dickens's most peculiar creations, and as powerfully drawn and painted as any portrait in any literature.

Listen to this: "There are people whom it is difficult to describe correctly in their typical and characteristic aspect. These are the people who are usually called 'the mass,' 'the majority,' and who do actually make up the vast majority of mankind. To this class of 'commonplace' or 'ordinary' people belong certain persons of my tale, such as Gavril Ardalionovitch."[1]

Now, this is a character particularly difficult to delineate. What will he succeed in telling us about him?

"A profound and continual consciousness of his own lack of talent, and at the same time the overwhelming desire to prove to himself that he was a man of great independence, had rankled in his heart from boyhood up. He was a young man of violent and envious cravings, who seemed to have been positively born with his nerves overwrought. The violence of his desires he took for strength. This passionate craving to distinguish himself sometimes led him to the brink of most ill-considered actions, but our hero was always at the last moment too sensible to take the final plunge. That drove him to despair."[2] And this for one of the least important characters in the book! I must add that the others, the chief protagonists, he does not portray, leaving them to limn in their own portrait, never finished, ever changing, in the course of the narrative. His principal characters are always in course of formation, never quite emerging from the shadows. In passing, note how profoundly different he is from Balzac, whose chief care seems ever to be the perfect consistency of his characters. Balzac paints like David; Dostoevsky like Rembrandt, and his protraits are artistically so powerful and often so perfect that even if they lacked the depths of thought that lie behind them, and around them, I believe that Dostoevsky would still be the greatest of all novelists.

[1] *The Idiot*, pp. 461–2.   [2] *Ibid*, p. 464.

DOSTOEVSKY IN HIS CORRESPONDENCE
(1908)

I

YOU are prepared to find a super-man: you lay hold on a fellow mortal, sick, poor, toiling without respite, and strangely lacking in that pseudo-quality he himself criticized so strongly in the French—eloquence. In dealing with a book so bare of all pretension, I shall hold remote every consideration save one, straightforwardness. If some there be who seek in these pages fine writing or intellectual entertainment, I warn them now, it were well to read no further.

The text of the letters is often confused, inaccurate, unskilfully put together, and we are grateful to Dostoevsky's translator for having renounced all idea of introducing a certain artificial elegance or attempting to remedy their characteristic awkwardness.[1]

The first contact is indeed discouraging. Mme Hoffmann, Dostoevsky's German biographer, leads us to understand that the selection of letters issued by the Russian editors might have been better made; but she entirely fails to convince me that its keynote could have been different. As it stands, the volume is bulky, and the reader gasps in astonishment less at the number of the letters than at the vast formlessness of each one of them. Perhaps we have never yet had an example of a literary man's letters so badly written, by that I mean written with so little regard for style. Ideas seem to come from his pen not in ordered sequence,

[1] M. Gide refers to J. W. Bienstock's translation, *Correspondance et Voyage à l'Étranger*, Paris, 1908. (*Translator's note.*

but in a rich confusion, which, once it is brought under control, contributes powerfully to the complexity of his novels. The same man who is so uncompromising and so tenacious where his own work is concerned, correcting, destroying, modifying his stories, page by page, until each becomes "the expression of his very being," writes his correspondence anyhow: never crossing a phrase out, but constantly catching himself up, hurrying on as fast as he can, and never able to bring his letter to a satisfactory close; and nothing helps us better to estimate the distance between a work and its creator. Inspiration? romantic and flattering convenience! The muse is not so readily wooed. And if ever Buffon's modest saying—"*A patience that knows no weariness*" —were applicable, 'tis here.

"What theory is this you've got hold of?" he writes to his brother, on the very threshold of his career.[1] "A picture ought to be painted at one sitting, you say! When did you acquire this conviction? Believe me, in all things, labour, yes, prolonged labour, is indispensable. A few lines of Pushkin's verse, light and polished, truly seem the fruit of one effort, thanks to the hours Pushkin spent arranging and revising them. It needs more than a happy knack to produce mature work. We are told that Shakespeare's work bears no trace of correction: that is exactly why we find in it so many imperfections and so much that is contrary to good taste. If he had spent more time over it, the result would have been better." Such is the keynote of the whole correspondence. The best of his life and spirit Dostoevsky devotes to his work. None of his letters was written from pleasure. He constantly reverts to his "terrible, unmasterable, incredible distaste for letter-writing."—"Letters," he declares, "have neither rhyme nor reason: it is impossible to unburden oneself in them." He goes even further: "I write

[1] Letter to his brother Michael, Semipalatinsk, May 31, 1858.

to you at great length, and I see that of the very essence of my moral or spiritual life I have given you not a notion, and so it will remain as long as we continue to correspond; I *cannot* write letters: I cannot write about myself and be just."[1] Elsewhere he says that "in a letter it's impossible to write anything. There's the secret of my dislike of Madame de Sévigné: the woman wrote her letters too well!" Or with a touch of humour: "If ever I go to the lower regions I shall beyond a doubt be sentenced to write for my sins some ten letters a day"—and I think this is the one flicker of humour you can discern throughout the whole gloomy book.

So only direst compulsion will drive him to write a letter. His correspondence (save during the last ten years of his life when the tone is altered—and of this period I shall speak apart) is one prolonged cry of distress: he is penniless, desperate, and he seeks help. A cry, did I say? It is one unending monotonous lament. He is a beggar, and does not know how to beg: he is all awkwardness, without pride, and innocent of irony. He reminds me of the angel of whom we read in the *Little Flowers of St Francis*. This angel, in the form of a traveller who had lost his way, came to the Val de Spolete and knocked at the door of the infant settlement. His knocking was so loud, long, and precipitate that the brethren grew indignant, and Brother Masseo (M. de Vogüé, I presume!) at last opened the door, asking, "Whence comest thou to knock in so unseemly wise?" And the angel inquired, "How then must I knock?" Brother Masseo replied, "Knock thrice with deliberation, then pause. Leave the porter time to say a pater-noster. Then if he comes not, knock again." "*But I am sore pressed,*" continued the angel.

"I am in such poverty that I am fit to hang myself,"

[1] Bienstock, p. 122. Letter to A. N. Maïkov, Semipalatinsk, January 18, 1856.

writes Dostoevsky, "I can neither pay my debts nor leave, lacking funds for the journey, and I am in black despair."— "What is to become of me between now and the close of the year? I don't know. My head is bursting. I have not a soul left from whom I can borrow."—("Do you realize what it means, to have nowhere to go?" says one of his characters.) "I've written to a relative to ask him for six hundred roubles. If he doesn't send them, then all is lost." His correspondence is so full of such laments and others in like strain that I make my selection at random. Sometimes there is, every six months or so, a note of greater insistence: "It is only once in a lifetime that money can possibly be so cruelly needed."

Towards the end—as if drunk with the humility with which he intoxicated the heroes of his novels, that uncanny Russian humility, which may be Christ-like, but which, according to Mme Hoffmann, is still to be found in the depths of every Russian soul even where Christian faith is lacking, and which the Western mind will never fully understand since it reckons self-respect a virtue—he asks, "Why should they deny me? I make no demands. I am but a humble petitioner!"

But perhaps these letters furnish, wrongly, the impression of a human creature ever deep in despair, seeing that they were written only when despair was greatest. No: incoming moneys were immediately swallowed up by debts, and thus, at the age of fifty, he could truthfully say of himself, "My life long I have toiled for money, and my life long I have been in need, more sorely now than ever."[1] Debts, or gambling, lack of restraint, and that instinctive, prodigal generosity which made Riesenkampf, the companion of his youth, say, "Dostoevsky is one of those people in whose company a man lives well, but who himself will remain a needy creature till the very end of his days."

When fifty, he wrote: "This plan of a novel (i.e. *The*

[1] Bienstock, p. 364. Letter to N. N. Strakhov, Dresden, February 26, 1870.

Brothers Karamazov, not written till nine years later) has been tormenting me now for more than three years; but I have not made a start with it, because I should like to write it in my own good time, like Tolstoy, Turgeniev, and Gontcharov. Let me write at least one of my works unhampered and without the preoccupation of being ready at a fixed date."[1] But it is in vain that he repeats, "I don't understand hurriedly done work, written for money": this money question invariably obtrudes itself, together with the fear of not being ready in time. "I dread not being ready in time, being late. I should hate to spoil things by my haste. I admit the plan has been well conceived and thought over; but haste can ruin all."[2]

The result of this is terrible overstrain, for he stakes his honour on an ideal of faithfulness that is beset with difficulties, and he would die in harness sooner than furnish imperfect work. Towards the close of his life he can say: "Throughout my literary career, I have kept my agreements with scrupulous exactness, not once have I broken my word; and what is more, I have never written for money's sake alone, nor in order to deliver myself from accepted obligations," and a little before, in the same letter: "I have never invented a theme for money's sake, to meet the obligation of writing up to a previously agreed time-limit. I always made an agreement . . . and sold myself into bondage beforehand . . . only when I already had my theme in mind prepared for writing, and when it was one that I felt it necessary to develop."[3] So if in one of his early letters (written at the age of twenty-four) he makes protest: "Whatever befall me, my resolution will remain unshaken; even if driven to the extreme limit of privation, I shall stand firm and never compose to order. Constraint is pernicious and

---

[1] Bienstock, pp. 387–8. Letter to N. N. Strakhov, Dresden, December 2, 1870.
[2] *Ibid.*, p. 415. Letter to A. N. Maïkov, Dresden, March 2, 1871.
[3] *Ibid.*, pp. 364–5. Letter to N. N. Strakhov, Dresden, February 26, 1870.

soul-destroying. I want each of my works to be good in itself"[1] . . . we can, without cavilling, admit that he did not break his vow.

But he cherished throughout his life the belief that with more time and freedom he could have given better expression to his thought. "There is one consideration that troubles one greatly: if I spent a year writing the novel beforehand, and then two or three months in copying and revising it, I guarantee the result would be very different." Self-delusion, maybe? Who can tell? With greater leisure, to what could he have attained? After what was he still striving? Greater simplicity, no doubt, and a more complete subordination of detail. As they are, his best works rise, almost throughout, to a degree of precision and clarity that it is not easy to imagine excelled.

And to reach this, what expenditure of effort! It is only now and again that sudden inspiration is vouchsafed; everything else means painful toil. To his brother, who doubtless had reproached him with not writing "simply" enough, meaning to say "quickly" enough, and with not "surrendering himself to inspiration," he replied, young as he was: "It is clear that you are confusing, as often happens, inspiration, that is, first momentary creation of the picture, or the stirring of the soul, with work. Thus, for instance, I make note at once of a scene just as it appeared to me, and I am delighted: then, for months, for a year even, I work at it . . . and believe me, the finished article is much superior. Provided, of course, that the inspiration is vouchsafed! Naturally without inspiration nothing can be accomplished. . . ." Must I crave pardon for this prodigality of quotation, or will you not rather be grateful to me for allowing Dostoevsky to be his own spokesman as much as possible? "At the beginning, that is at the end of last year, I thought the novel (he refers

[1] Bienstock, p. 55. Letter to his brother Michael, March 24, 1845.

to *The Possessed*) very *made* and artificial and rather scorned it. But later I was overtaken by real enthusiasm. I fell in love with my work of a sudden, and made a big effort to get all that I had written into good trim. . . ."[1] "The whole year," he goes on to say (1870), "I have done nothing but destroy. . . . I have altered my plan at least ten times, and I've re-written the first part entirely. Two or three months ago I was in despair. Now everything has fallen into place together and cannot be changed." And again the ever-present obsession: "If I had had time to write without hurrying myself, without a time-limit in view, it is possible that something good might have developed out of it."[2]

This anguish and this dissatisfaction with himself were gone through for every work that he wrote. "It is a long novel, in six parts (*Crime and Punishment*). At the end of November a large part of it was written and ready; I burned the lot! Now I can frankly admit that it did not please me. A new form, a new plan hurried me along. I have made a fresh start. I am working night and day; still, progress is slow."—"I am working hard and little comes of it," he says elsewhere: "I am constantly tearing my work up. I am terribly discouraged." And again: "I have done so much work that I've become stupid, and my head is dazed."— "I am working here (Staraia Roussa) like a convict in spite of the fine weather to be taken advantage of; I am tied night and day to my task."

Sometimes a mere article gives him as much trouble as a book, because his conscientiousness is as rigid in little things as in great.

"I have let it drag on till now" (i.e. a memoir on Bielinsky, which has not been traced), "and at last I've finished it,

---

[1] Mayne, p. 198. Letter to N. N. Strakhov, Dresden, October 9, 1870.

[2] Bienstock, pp. 386–7. Letter to N. N. Strakhov, Dresden, December 2, 1870.

gnashing my teeth the while. Ten pages of a novel are more easily written than these two sheets. Consequently I've written, all in all, this confounded article five times at least, and even then I've scored everything out and changed what I'd written. Finally I've completed the article after a fashion, but it is so bad that I am full of disgust."[1] For while he clings to the profound belief in his worth, in the worth of his ideas at least, he is always exacting while the work is in progress, and never pleased when it is completed.

"I've seldom happened to have anything newer, more complete or more original. I can say this without being accused of pride, because I am speaking of the subject only, of the idea that has sprung up in my head, and not of its realization; as for the latter, it lies with God. I can make a complete mess of it—which has happened before to-day."

"However wretched and abominable what I've written may be," he says in another passage, "the idea of the novel and the labour I expend on it are to me, its unhappy author, my most precious possession in life."

"My dissatisfaction with my novel amounts to disgust," so he writes when working at *The Idiot*. "I have made a terrible effort to work, but simply could not; my heart is bad. Just now I am making a last effort for the third part. If I succeed in polishing off this book, I'll get better: if not, it is all over with me."

Having already written not only the three books M. de Vogüé reckons his masterpieces, but *Notes from Underground*, *The Idiot*, and *The Eternal Husband*, he concentrates all his efforts on a new theme (*The Possessed*), exclaiming, "It's high time I wrote something serious."

And the year of his death, writing to Mlle N——, he says: "I am conscious that, as a writer, I have many defects,

[1] Bienstock, p. 267. Letter to A. N. Maïkov, Geneva, September 15, 1867.

because I am the first to be dissatisfied with my own efforts. You can just picture the times when I cross-examine myself, to find that I have literally not expressed the twentieth part of what was in my mind, and could, perhaps, have been expressed! My salvation lies in the sure hope that one day God may grant me such strength and inspiration that I shall find perfect self-expression and be able to make plain all that I carry in my heart and imagination."[1]

How remote from Balzac with his self-assurance and rich imperfection! Can even Flaubert have known what it is to make such demands upon oneself, to struggle so hard and toil in such mad frenzies? I think not. His exigencies are more purely literary, and if his uncompromising uprightness as a writer and the tale of his prodigious labours are prominently displayed in his letters, it is simply because he becomes attached to this very labour, and without exactly vaunting it, he is at least uncommonly proud of it. Besides, he suppressed all else, holding life so "loathsome a thing, that the only way to bear it is to avoid it," and compared himself to the "Amazons who cut off their breasts, the better to bend the bow." Dostoevsky suppressed nothing; he had a wife and children, whom he adored, and life he did not scorn. After his release from prison, he wrote: "At least, I have lived; I have suffered, but I have lived!" His sacrifices for love of his art are the nobler and the more tragic because less arrogant, less conscious, less deliberate. He frequently quotes Terence, refusing to concede that anything human should be foreign to himself either. "Man has not the right to turn aside and heed not what is happening in the world around him, and this I maintain on moral grounds of the highest order. Homo sum, et nihil humanum. . . ." He does not despise his suffering, but assumes the burden in all

[1] Bienstock, pp. 470-1. Letter to Mlle N. N——, Petersburg, April 11, 1880.

its fullness. Losing wife and brother within the space of a few months, he writes: "And then I was suddenly left alone, and I knew fear! It has become terrible. My life broken in two! On one hand, the past, with all that I had to live for, on the other, the unknown, with not one loving heart to comfort me in my loss. There was literally no reason why I should go on living. Forge new links, start a fresh existence? The very thought revolted me! I realized then for the first time that I could not replace my lost ones, they were all I held dear, and new loves could not, ought not to exist."[1] But a fortnight later, this is what he wrote: "Of all my reserves of strength and energy, there is nothing left save a vague uneasiness of soul, a state bordering on despair. Bitterness and indecision—a mood foreign to me. And then I'm utterly alone. Yet I always have the feeling that I am going to begin to live! Ridiculous, isn't it? The cat and its nine lives?"[2] He was at this moment forty-four years of age, and less than a year later, he married a second time.

At twenty-eight years of age, confined in a fortress pending transfer to Siberia, he cried, "I see I have within me resources of vitality that it will be hard to exhaust." And in 1856, still in Siberia, but released from prison, and not long married to a widow, Marie Dimitrievna Issaïev by name, he wrote: "Now things are different from what they used to be! So much more reflection, effort and energy enters into my work. Can it be that after struggling so resolutely and courageously for six long years I am incapable of earning enough money to support my wife and myself? Impossible! Nobody knows yet the worth of my powers or the extent of my talent, and this is what I chiefly count on!"

But, alas! he has to struggle against other ills than poverty.

[1] Bienstock, p. 235. Letter to Baron Alexander Wrangel, Petersburg, March 31, 1865.

[2] Ibid., p. 239. Letter to Baron Alexander Wrangel, Petersburg, April 9, 1865.

"My work is done in care and suffering, and I am always at high nervous tension. When I do too much, I become physically ill."—"Of late I've been working literally day and night, in spite of my attacks." And again: "These attacks will make an end of me: after one, it takes me four days to straighten out my thoughts."

Dostoevsky was never reticent concerning his epilepsy; his attacks of the *falling sickness* were, alas! all too frequent not to have been witnessed at times by some of his intimates, aye, and by strangers too. Strakhov describes one of these fits in his *Reminiscences*, unconscious, as the sufferer himself was, that there could be the slightest shame attached to the epileptic condition, or that it implied any moral or intellectual "inferiority" apart from the resultant hindrances to work. Even to correspondents of the other sex who were personally unknown to him and whom he was addressing for the first time, he would apologize for his delay in writing, with the naïve and simple remark: "I have just had three of my epileptic fits, uncommonly violent and in rapid succession. But after the attacks, for two or three days I was unable to work, write, or even read, because I am a wreck, body and soul. So now I've told you, and I ask your forgiveness for leaving you so long without a reply."

This disease, from which he suffered even before Siberia, grew worse during his imprisonment; it abated but very little during an occasional stay abroad, renewing its force as soon as he returned home. Sometimes the interval between the attacks is longer, but this only augments their violence. "When the fits are infrequent and one suddenly comes over me, I am subject to blackest melancholy. I am reduced to despair. Formerly (he was fifty when he wrote this) this mood lasted three days after the attack, nowadays, a week or more."

Braving his attacks, he holds fast to his work, making

huge efforts to implement his promises: "The next instal-
ment (of *The Idiot*) is announced for April, and I've nothing
ready, except one unimportant chapter. What am I to send?
I have no idea. The day before yesterday I did some writing
all the same, in a state bordering on madness."

If the sole consequence were pain and discomfort! But,
alas! "I notice to my despair that I am no longer fit to work
as quickly as of old, indeed, as up till quite recently." Again
and again he laments the weakening of his memory and his
imagination, and at the age of fifty-eight, two years before
his death, he said: "For a long time I've been conscious that
where work is concerned, the longer, the more difficult, and
so my thoughts are gloomy, and there is nowhere solace for
me." And yet, he could write *The Karamazovs*.

When Baudelaire's *Letters* were published last year, M.
Mendès was shocked and protested, in no measured terms
either, invoking the poet's right to have his intimate
concerns respected.

No doubt there will always be ultra-sensitive, easily
shocked readers who prefer to see only the heads and
shoulders of great men, who rise up in revolt at the publication of personal documents and private correspondence,
discerning in these only what can agreeably flatter a
mediocre intelligence which delights to find a hero bound by
the same infirmities as itself. So they talk of "indiscretion";
or if they are of a romantic turn of mind, of "ghouls"; at the
mildest, of "unhealthy curiosity." "Leave the man in peace,"
they say, "his work alone is of account." Agreed! but the
wonder of it, and, to me, the profound lesson of it, is, that
the "work" should have been written in spite of the "man".

I am not writing Dostoevsky's biography, I am merely
drawing his likeness from the elements of his *Correspondence*,
so I have discussed only the difficulties engendered by his
very constitution. I think I am justified in including

amongst them his chronic poverty, so intimately connected with him that it would seem to have met some secret need of his being. . . . But everything goes against him; at the outset of his career, in spite of his delicacy in childhood, he is pronounced fit for military service, whereas his brother, Michael, more robust in health, is rejected. Straying into a group of political suspects, he is arrested, condemned to death, then respited and sent to Siberia to expiate his offence. He spends ten years there: four in prison, six at Semipalatinsk in a regiment of the line. While there he married; perhaps not very much "in love" according to our usual interpretation of the phrase, but out of a kind of burning compassion, out of pity or softened feeling, out of a need for sacrificing himself and a natural propensity for assuming burdens and shirking no issue. His wife was the widow of a prisoner, Issaïev, and the mother of a growing boy (a good-for-nothing, almost mentally defective), who there and then became dependent upon Dostoevsky. In a letter to his friend Wrangel, after his wife's death, he wrote: "Ah, dear friend, she loved me deeply, and I returned her love; yet, we did not live happily together. I shall tell you all about it when I see you. Let me say just this, although we were unhappy (by reason of her difficult character—she was hypochondriac, and full of a sick woman's whims), we could not cease to love each other. Indeed, the unhappier we became, the more closely we drew together. Strange though it may seem, it's true!". "If you question me about myself, what can I say? I have family cares, and they press heavily. But I believe my day is not done, and I am determined not to die," he says elsewhere. After his brother Michael's death, he has to support his family too. As soon as he puts some money aside—which means the possibility of some respite —he starts newspapers and reviews,[1] at once financing and

[1] "To defend the theories he fancies are his," says M. de Vogüé.

editing the publications. "Energetic measures were imperative. I started publications with three different presses, and
I have spared neither money, health, nor efforts. I ran everything singlehanded. I revised proofs, kept in touch with the
authors and with the Censorship, found the necessary
money. I was up till six in the morning, and took only five
hours sleep. I at last managed to put the review on its feet,
but too late." As a matter of fact, this review *did* collapse.
"But the worst of it," he continues, "was, that working like
a galley-slave at these concerns, I could not write anything
for the review: not a line from *my* pen. My name was never in
the public's eye, and not only in the provinces, but in Petersburg even, it was not known that I was the editor."

He persists in spite of everything, and makes a fresh
start; nothing can discourage him or bring him down. In the
last year of his life, however, he is still struggling, not
against public opinion which he has at length won over, but
against opposition papers. "For what I said in Moscow (his
speech on 'Pushkin'), just look how I've been treated by
almost the whole of the press: it is as if I were a thief or had
embezzled from some bank or other. Ukhantsev (a notorious
swindler of the time) is less foully abused than I."

But it is not a reward that he is seeking, any more than it is
amour-propre or author's vanity that inspires his conduct.
Nothing could be more significant than his manner of accep-
ting his first success: "I've been writing three years already,
and it dazes me; I am not living. I haven't time to think. . . .
A precarious reputation has been built up round me, and
I don't know how long the damnable thing will last."

He is so persuaded of the worth of his ideas that personal
values are absorbed and lost. "What have I done", he wrote
to his friend, Baron Wrangel, "that you should bestow such
affection upon me?" And near the close of his life, writing to
an anonymous correspondent: "Do you think I am one of

those who mend hearts, deliver the soul, and drive out suffering? Many people write to tell me this, but I am certain I am more capable of provoking disillusion and disgust. I have little skill in healing, although I have sometimes tried it." Such love in this tormented soul! "I dream of you every night," he writes from Siberia to his brother, "and I am terribly worried. I do not want you to die; I must see you and kiss you again, my dear. Allay my fears, for the love of God; for the love of Christ, if you are well, forget your business and your worries, and write to me at once, immediately, else I shall go mad."[1]

Is there any help for him, this time at least? "Write to me at once and in detail how you found my brother," he writes from Semipalatinsk, on March 23, 1856, to Baron Wrangel: "What does he think about me? He used to love me passionately. He wept when he bade me good-bye. Has his feeling towards me grown cold? Has his character changed? That would be a grief. Has he forgotten all the past? I cannot believe it, but how else am I to explain his not writing for seven or eight months? And I seem to see so little warmth in him to remind me of days gone by! I shall never forget what he said to K—— who delivered my message entreating him to exert himself on my behalf: '*The best thing for him to do is to remain in Siberia.*' " He actually wrote these words, but he would give anything to forget his brother's cruelty. The affectionate letter to Michael from which I quoted a moment ago is subsequent to this one.

During his four years in prison Dostoevsky was left without news of his family. On February 22, 1854, ten days before his liberation, he wrote to his brother the first of the Siberian letters preserved to us, an admirable letter, regrettably not in Bienstock: "At last I can talk with you somewhat more explicitly, and, I believe, in a more

[1] Bienstock, p. 159. To his brother Michael, Semipalatinsk, July 19, 1858.

reasonable manner. But before I write another line I *must* ask you: tell me, for God's sake, why you have never written me a single syllable till now? Could I have expected this from you? Believe me, in my lonely and isolated state, I sometimes fell into utter despair, for I believed that you were no longer alive; through whole nights I would brood upon what was to become of your children, and I cursed my fate because I could not help them. . . ."[1]—"Can you possibly have been forbidden to write to me? Because writing *is* actually permitted! All the political prisoners have several letters each year. . . . But I think I have guessed the true cause of your silence: it is your natural apathy."

"'Tell my brother", he wrote later to Wrangel, "that I fold him in my arms, that I ask his forgiveness for all the pain I've caused him, and kneel at his feet";[2] and to his brother himself, on August 21, 1855: "Dear brother, when in my letter of last October I repeated my complaints at your silence, you answered that these had made very painful reading for you. Oh, Mysha! for the love of God, bear me no ill-will; remember my loneliness. I am like a pebble cast aside. I've always been of a gloomy, sickly, susceptible disposition; remember all that, and forgive me if my reproaches were unjust and my fancies absurd. I am myself thoroughly convinced I was in the wrong."

Mme Hoffmann was right, no doubt, and Western readers will protest in face of such humility and contrition. Our literature, too often tinged with Castillian pride, has so thoroughly taught us to see nobility of character in the non-forgiveness of injury and insult!

But what will he have to say, the Western-European reader, when he reads this: "You write that everybody loves

<hr>

[1] Mayne, p. 51.

[2] Bienstock, p. 135. Letter to Baron Alexander Wrangel, Semipalatinsk, May 23, 1856.

the Tsar. I venerate him."? And Dostoevsky was still in Siberia when he wrote these words. Irony, perchance? No. In letter after letter he takes up the theme: "The Emperor is infinitely generous and kind." And this is what he says when, after ten years' imprisonment, he solicits permission to return to Petersburg and a place for his stepson, Paul, at the Gymnasium: "I have been thinking if one request is refused, maybe the other will be granted, and if the Emperor does not think fit to allow me to live in Petersburg, perhaps he will agree to find an opening for Paul, so that his refusal will not be absolute."

Decidedly, submissiveness to this degree is disconcerting! Nothing here for nihilists, anarchists, or even socialists, to use for their own ends. What! not a cry of revolt? Perhaps it was prudent to show respect for the Tsar, but why no revolt against society, or against the prison-cell from which he emerged an aged man? Just listen to what he says about his prison, in a letter to Michael dated February 22, 1856: "What has happened to my soul and my beliefs, my intellect and my affections in the space of these four years, I shall not tell you! The tale would be too long. The unbroken meditation, wherein I found refuge from the bitterness of reality, has surely not been vain. I now have hopes and desires which in bygone days I did not even anticipate." And in another passage: "Do not imagine, I pray you, that I am still as moody and suspicious as I was in my last years in Petersburg. All that has gone for ever. God, too, is leading us." And not long after, in another letter to S. D. Janovsky in 1872,[1] we come across this extraordinary confession (the italics are Dostoevsky's!): "You loved me, cared for me, and I was then *sick in mind* (I realize it now) *before my journey to Siberia*, where I was cured."

No single word of protest! On the contrary, nothing

[1] Bienstock, p. 438.

but gratitude: Like Job, who uttered no blasphemy in his heart when smitten by the hand of the Ancient of Days. . . . An unrewarding martyr. In what faith does he live and move? What are the convictions that lend him strength?

Perhaps an examination of his *opinions*, so far as his letters make them plain, will help us to understand the secret causes, already faintly indicated, of his disfavour and *lack of success* with the public, and explain why Dostoevsky still lingers on, as if in purgatory, in a middle state between obscurity and fame.

DOSTOEVSKY was no partisan. Dreading party feeling and the dissensions it creates, he wrote: "My thoughts are chiefly concerned with what constitutes our community of ideas, the common ground whereon we all might meet, irrespective of tendency." Profoundly convinced that "in Russian thought lay reconciliation for Europe's antagonisms", "veteran European Russian" as he termed himself, he devoted the whole strength of his being to the Russian unity which was to confound party and faction in one great love of country and of humanity. "Yes, I too hold your opinion that in Russia, by the very nature of her mission, Europe will be consummated. This has long been plain to me," so he wrote from Siberia. Elsewhere he describes Russia as "a nation awaiting her mission", "fit to lead the common interests of entire humanity." And if, by virtue of a conviction which, perchance, was no more than premature, he deceived himself as to the importance of the Russian people (which is by no means *my* opinion), it was not infatuated jingoism, but his intuition and the deep understanding he had, simply because he himself was a Russian, of the beliefs and party passions dividing Europe. Speaking of Pushkin, he credits himself with the poet's "gift of world-wide sympathy," adding, "It is this very faculty, his in common with all our people, which makes him truly national." He considers the Russian soul as "a meeting-ground whereon all European aims may be reconciled", exclaiming, "Where is the true Russian who does not first and foremost think of Europe?" and uttering even these strange words, "the Russian wanderer has need of world-wide happiness in order to find peace himself."

Persuaded that "Russia's future activity must be in the highest degree pan-human", and that "maybe the Russian idea will be the synthesis of all the ideas developed with such courage and persistence in the various European nationalities", his gaze is constantly directed outside Russia. His political and social judgments of France and of Germany are, to us, perhaps the most interesting passages of his correspondence. He travelled abroad, lingering in Italy, Switzerland, and Germany, attracted in the first instance by his desire to know them, detained ultimately for months on end by the eternal question of money, either having an insufficiency of funds to continue his journey or fearing debts he has left behind in Russia, and the possibility of tasting imprisonment again. "With my health in the state it is," he wrote when he was forty-nine, "I could not stand even six months' confinement, nor, what is more, could I work."

But in foreign parts he misses from the very first the air of Russia and the contact with the Russian people. For him, Sparta, Toledo and Venice might as well not exist, he cannot become acclimatized, nor can he content himself anywhere for a moment. "I have no words to tell you how unbearable living abroad is to me," he writes to his friend Strakhov. Not a letter written in exile but breathes the same lament: "I *must* go back to Russia; the monotony of life here is crushing." And as though in Russia were hidden the source of nourishment for his work, and the sap failed as soon as he was torn from his native soil, he wrote: "I have no taste for writing, or else, when I do write, it is with much suffering. I cannot think what this means, except it be that I have need of Russia, to work and to create. . . . I was only too clearly conscious that whether we lived at Dresden or elsewhere was a matter of indifference, for I should always be a foreigner in a foreign land." Again: "If only you knew how good-for-nothing and alien I feel here. I am growing stupid and dull, and am losing touch with Russia. No breath of Russian air, no Russian spirit. I don't understand the Russian exiles: madmen all!"

And yet at Geneva, at Vevey, he wrote *The Idiot*, at Dresden *The Eternal Husband* and *The Possessed*. "You have spoken golden words about my work here. Right enough, I shall fall behind, not behind the times, but I shall lose touch with what is happening at home (I know it better than you do, because *every day* of my life I read three Russian newspapers, every line of them, and I receive a couple of reviews), I shall become deaf to the *living pulse of life;* and how that tells on artistic creation!"

So this "world sympathy" exists together with and is strengthened by an ardent nationalism—its natural complement in Dostoevsky's mind. He never wearies or flags in his protest against those that were at that time called the "Progressists," that is to say (I borrow this definition from Strakhov), "the generation of politicians which expected the advancement of Russian civilization to proceed not from an organic development of the national character, but from an overhasty assimilation of Western teachings." "The Frenchman is first and foremost a Frenchman, and an Englishman an Englishman, and their highest aim is to remain true to themselves. Therein lies their strength." He takes his stand against the "men who seek to uproot the Russians," and does not wait for Barrès to warn the young intellectual "who tears himself away from society and disowns it, and does not 'go to the people,' but loses himself in foreign parts, in 'Europeanism,' in the kingdom of the universal man who has never existed, and in so doing breaks with the people, scorns it and misjudges it." Like Barrès dealing with "sickly Kantism", he writes in the preface to the review[1] he edits:

[1] See Bienstock, pp. 592–8: Preface to *The Epoch*, 1865.

"No matter how fertile an idea imported from abroad, it can only strike root here, become acclimatized, and prove of genuine use to us if our national life, spontaneously and without pressure from without, made the idea grow up, naturally and practically, to meet its own needs—needs which have been recognized by practical experience. No nation on earth, no society with a certain measure of stability has been developed to order, on the lines of a programme imported from abroad."

Here follows a remark I regret not to have found in Barrès: "The capacity for separating oneself temporarily from one's mother-earth for the purposes of self-contemplation, all prejudices apart, is the mark of a very strong personality, just as the power to look on the foreigner with kindly eyes is one of nature's highest and noblest gifts." And did Dostoevsky not seem to foresee how this doctrine was to lead and blind us?—"It is impossible to undeceive a Frenchman and prevent his believing himself the most important being in the wide world. Besides, of the wide world he is pretty ignorant. And what is more, he is not keen to be enlightened. This is a characteristic common to the whole nation, and very typical."

Dostoevsky's individualism, too, differentiates him more sharply—and more happily—from Barrès. And, set against Nietzsche, he becomes for us a shining example of how little infatuation and self-sufficiency may at times accompany belief in the value of the personality. "The hardest thing on earth," he writes, "is to remain yourself," and "no high aim is worth a life wrecked," because for him, without individualism as without patriotism, there exists no way of serving humanity. If some Barrès enthusiasts were won over to him by the declarations I quoted a moment ago, is there one of them who would not be alienated by these fresh statements?

So, too, on reading these words: "In the new humanity,

the æsthetic idea lacks clarity. The moral basis of society, held fast by positivism, not only gives no results, but cannot define itself, for it is lost in cloudy aspirations and ideals. Are there yet not enough facts to prove that society is not established thus, that these are not the paths leading to happiness, and that this is not, as has been believed till now, the source of happiness? But what *is* its source then? So many volumes are written, and the essential point is ever missed: the Western World has lost Christ Jesus—and for this, and this alone, the Western World must perish." Not a French Catholic but would applaud—were he not drawn up sharply by the phrase I dropped at the beginning: "Christ has been lost, by the error of Catholicism."

What French Catholic will now dare let himself be touched by the tears of devotion that are shed throughout these letters of Dostoevsky's? Vain hope, "to desire to reveal to the world a Russian Christ, unknown to the wider world, whose very being is contained in our orthodoxy."

The French Catholic by virtue of his own personal orthodoxy, will refuse to listen, and for the moment, at least, Dostoevsky's further remark is made in vain: "In my opinion, here is found the principle of our future civilizing force and of Europe's resurrection at our hands, the very essence of our future strength."

Although Dostoevsky gives M. de Vogüé grounds for discerning in him a "bitter animosity against thought and against life in its fullness," a "sanctification of the mindless, colourless, and invertebrate," and so on, we read in another passage from a letter to his brother: "Simple folk, you will say. Aye, but I dread simple men more than complex ones."[1] This was his reply to a girl who "was anxious to make herself useful," and had expressed her desire to become a mid-wife or hospital nurse: "By giving regular attention to your

[1] Mayne, p. 62.

general education you will fit yourself for an activity more useful a hundred times. Would it not be better to give thought to the higher branches of your general education? . . . The majority of our specialists are fundamentally ignorant—and most of our students, of both sexes, are absolutely uneducated. What good can *they* do to humanity?"[1] Frankly I did not need these words to realize M. de Vogüé's mistake; but all the same, this mistake *was* possible.

Dostoevsky is not any more easily enrolled "for" or "against" Socialism; for, if Mme Hoffmann is justified in saying, "A Socialist, in the most human acceptation of the word, Dostoevsky never for a moment ceased to be!" do we not read in his letters, "Socialism has already undermined Europe: if we delay too long, it will bring it to complete ruin"?

Conservative, but not hide-bound by tradition: monarchist, but of democratic opinions: Christian, but not a Roman Catholic: liberal, but not a progressive: Dostoevsky remains ever the man of whom *there is no way to make use!* He is of the stuff which displeases every party. Why? Because he never persuaded himself that less than the whole of his intelligence was necessary to the part he chose to play, or that for the sake of immediate issues he would be justified in forcing so delicate an instrument or upsetting its balance. "À propos of all *these possible tendencies*," he wrote (and the italics are his own), "which were united in an expression of welcome to me (April 9, 1876),[2] I should gladly have written an article on the impression made by the letters, but, on reflection, I realized that it would be impossible to write it in all sincerity: now, lacking sincerity, could it be worth

---

[1] Bienstock, pp. 447–8. Letter to Mlle Guérassimov, Petersburg, March 7, 1877.

[2] *Ibid.*, p. 442. Letter to Mme C. D. Altschevsky, Petersburg, April 9, 1876.

while?" What does he mean? Doubtless this: to write a reasonable article so as to please everybody and make a success of it, he would have to strain his ideas, simplify them to excess, in short, force his convictions beyond *natural limits*. And that is just what he cannot concede.

His individualism, while not harsh, and in reality one with his honesty of thought, does not allow him to submit his idea unless in its integrity, complex though this may be. And there is no stronger or subtler reason for his unpopularity amongst us.

I do not mean to insinuate that strong convictions ordinarily involve a certain dishonesty in reasoning; but they *do* willingly dispense with intelligence. And yet, M. Barrès is too clever not to have quickly grasped the fact that not by impartial illumination of all its aspects can we ensure the speedy dissemination of an idea, but by giving it a definite bias.

If you want ideas to succeed, you must submit them one at a time; or, better, to succeed, submit one idea and no more. It is not enough to invent a good medium of expression; it is a question of never outgrowing it. The public likes to know exactly where it stands when a great name is mentioned. And tolerates ill what would congest its brain! At the mention of Pasteur, it likes to be able to say to itself, without hesitation: Yes, hydrophobia. Nietzsche? the *superman*. Curie? radium. Barrès? France and her dead. Quinton? plasma. Just as if you were to say. Lazenby? pickles. And Parmentier, if so be it that he did "invent" the potato, is better known, thanks to this solitary vegetable, than if we had to thank him for the entire produce of our kitchen gardens.

Dostoevsky all but reached success in France, when M. de Vogüé had the bright idea of calling, and thus stereotyping in this handy phrase—*the religion of suffering*—the doctrine he found worked into the closing chapters of *Crime and Punishment*.

That it is there, I am willing to concede; also that the phrase was a happy invention. . . . Unfortunately it did not contain the whole being of the man: he was too great in every way to be compressed into such small bulk. For if he was of those for whom "only one thing is needful: to know God," at least this knowledge of God he tried to diffuse throughout his works in all its human and anxious complexity.

Ibsen was not easy to pin down either; like any other writer whose work is interrogative rather than affirmative. The relative success of the two plays, *A Doll's House* and *An Enemy of the People*, is due, certainly not to their outstanding excellence, but to the shadow of a conclusion which escaped Ibsen in them both. The public is but ill-pacified by the author who does not come to a strikingly evident solution. In its eyes, it is the sin of uncertainty, indolence of mind, lukewarmness of convictions. And most often, having little liking for intelligence, the public gauges the strength of a conviction by naught but the violence, persistence, and uniformity of the affirmation.

Anxious not to extend a field already so vast, I shall not attempt to define his doctrine here; I merely wanted to indicate its wealth of contradictions to the Western mind, unused to this need of reconciling extremes. Dostoevsky remains steadfast in the belief that between nationalism and europeanism, individualism and self-abnegation, the contradiction is apparent only. He holds that because each understands but one aspect of this vital question, the opposing parties remain uniformly remote from the truth. One more quotation: it will, I am sure, throw more light on Dostoevsky's position than any commentary. "To be happy must one be impersonal? Does salvation lie in self-effacement? Far from it, I should say. Not only must there be no self-effacement, but one must become a personality, even in a degree beyond what is possible in the West. Be clear as to my meaning: voluntary sacrifice, offered consciously and without constraint, sacrifice of the individual for the good of mankind, is, to my mind, the mark of personality in its noblest and highest development, of perfect self-control . . . the absolute expression of the will. A strongly developed personality, conscious of its right to be such, having cast out fear, cannot use itself, cannot be used, except in sacrifice for others, that these may become, like unto itself, self-determining and happy personalities. It is Nature's law, and mankind tends to reach it."[1] This solution is taught him by Christ: *"For whosoever will save his life shall lose it; but whosoever shall lose his life for My sake and the gospel's, the same shall save it."*

Back in Petersburg in the winter of 1871–2, being then fifty years of age, he writes to Janovsky:[2] "There is no use hiding the fact that old age is coming near, and yet one doesn't think of it, and makes preparation for a new work (*The Karamazovs*), for at last publishing something that will please; one still hopes for something out of life, and yet it is possible that everything has already been received. I am speaking of myself! Well, I am thoroughly happy!" This is the happiness, the joy beyond suffering latent in all Dostoevsky's life and work, a joy that Nietzsche had rightly sensed, and which I charge M. de Vogüé with having missed entirely.

The tone of the letters changes brusquely at this period. His usual correspondents being, like himself, in Petersburg, he is no longer writing to them but to strangers, chance correspondents who turn to him for edification, comfort, guidance. I should require to quote almost all the letters: my

[1] Bienstock, p. 540
Ibid., p. 437. Letter to S. D. Janovsky, Petersburg, February 4, 1872.

better plan is to refer you to the book; I am writing this
article solely to bring my reader into touch with it.

At last, freed from his horrible financial worries, he busies
himself during the closing years of his life with editing the
Journal of an Author, published only at irregular intervals.
"I confess," he wrote to the well-known Aksakov in
November, 1880 (that is, three months before his death),
"I confess in all friendship, that intending to undertake next
year the publication of the *Journal*, I have besought God
often and long to make me pure in heart and pure of lips;
without sin or envy, and incapable of wounding."[1]

In this *Journal* wherein M. de Vogüé could see only
"obscure pæans, evading alike analysis and discussion," the
Russian people happily discovered something different, and
Dostoevsky was able to feel that round about his work his
dream of spiritual harmony was almost being realized, without any arbitrary unification.

When his death was announced, this communion and
blending of spirits was shiningly manifested, and if, at first,
"subversive elements planned to monopolize his dead
body," very soon, "by the miracle of one of these unexpected fusions that are Russia's secret, when a national
conviction rouses her, all parties, all antagonists, all scattered
fragments of the empire were seen to be joined in a fresh
bond of enthusiasm by this death." The sentence is M. de
Vogüé's, and I rejoice after all the strictures I have made
concerning his study, to be able to quote such noble words.
"As it was said of the Tsars of old, that they gathered
together the land of Russia," he says later, "this spiritual
King had 'gathered together' the heart of Russia."

The same rallying of individual energies is at work now
throughout Europe, slowly, mysteriously, almost—chiefly

[1] Bienstock, p. 479. Letter to I. S. Aksakov, Petersburg, November 4,
1880.

in Germany, where the editions of his works are multiplying, in France, too, where the rising generation recognizes
and appreciates, better than that of M. de Vogüé's, his
strength. The hidden reasons which delayed his success will
be the builders of a more enduring fame.

ADDRESSES

(1922)

I

SOME time before the war I was preparing for Charles Péguy's *Cahiers de la Quinzaine*, a *Life of Dostoevsky* after the manner of Romain Rolland's fine monographs on Beethoven and Michelangelo. War came, and I was forced to lay aside the notes I had taken. For long other cares and duties absorbed me and my project was to all intents and purposes abandoned, when recently at the celebration of Dostoevsky's Centenary, Jacques Copeau asked me to address a meeting in his theatre, the *Vieux Colombier*. I brought my packet of notes out into the light of day again, and re-reading them after the lapse of time, I found the ideas I had jotted down seemed worth our attention, but that chronological order, though necessary for biographical purposes, was perhaps not the most advisable on this occasion. It is often a difficult task to separate the ideas Dostoevsky weaves, as it were, into a fine web in each of his novels, but we never lose track of them. In my eyes these ideas are all that is most precious in Dostoevsky and I have made them my own. If I took up each of his works in turn, I could not possibly avoid repeating myself. There is, however, another—and better—way: pursuing his ideas from one novel to another, I shall try to lay hold of them and set them forth as plainly as is possible despite their apparent confusion. Psychologist, sociologist, moralist—Dostoevsky is all three, and novelist as well. Whereas in his works ideas are never presented in their crude state, but always through the medium of the character expressing them (which accounts for their confusion and relativity), I, for my part, will try to avoid abstractions and outline the ideas as sharply as possible. I should like first of all to introduce you to Dostoevsky in person, and speak of some incidents in his life that reveal his character and help us to draw a clear likeness of him.

My pre-war plan of the biography comprised an introduction in which I proposed to discuss the commonly accepted idea of him. To throw light on the subject, I should have drawn a parallel between him and Rousseau—and no arbitrary one, I can assure you. Their natures reveal such deep-laid analogies that Rousseau's *Confessions* were able to exert an extraordinary influence on Dostoevsky. But in my opinion Rousseau, from the very beginning of his life, was poisoned, as it were, by Plutarch, through whom he fashioned for himself a somewhat rhetorical and pompous notion of a "great man." He set up before himself the image of a fancied hero, and his life was one prolonged effort to be like it. He tried hard to *be* what he wanted to *seem*. I allow that his painting of his own character may be sincere, but he is ever thinking of his pose, which pride alone dictates.

"False greatness," in the admirable words of La Bruyère, "is shy and inaccessible. Conscious of its foible, it hides away, or at least never shows an open face, letting be seen only as much as will make an impression and save it from being revealed for what it really is, something mean and small."

And if I do not go so far as to recognize Rousseau in this description, I *do* think of Dostoevsky when a little farther on I read:

"True greatness is free, gentle, familiar, unaffected; it can be touched and handled, and loses nothing when seen at close quarters. The better you are acquainted with it, the more you admire it. It bends out of goodness of heart to its inferiors, and returns to its own level without effort. Sometimes it lets itself go, neglecting and surrendering its natural advantages, but ever ready to recover them and put them to use."

With Dostoevsky there is this complete absence of pose or stage-management. He never considers himself a *superman*. He is most humbly human, and I do not think that pride of intellect could ever properly understand him.

The word *humility* comes up again and again in his letters and works. "Why should they deny me? I make no demands. I am but a humble petitioner." (November 23, 1869.)— "I do not demand, I only seek in all humility." (December 7, 1869.)—"I have made the humblest of requests." (February 12, 1870.)

"He often astonished me by a kind of humility," says the *Raw Youth* in speaking to his father, and in his effort to understand the possible relations between his father and mother, and the quality of their love, he recollects his father's phrase, "She married me out of humility."

I read lately in an interview with M. Henry Bordeaux a sentence which surprised me somewhat: "Seek first to know yourself." The literary creator who seeks himself runs a great risk—the risk of finding himself. From then onwards he writes coldly, deliberately, in keeping with the self he has found. He imitates himself. If he knows his path and his limitations, it is only to keep strictly to them. His great dread is no longer insincerity, but inconsistency. The true artist is never but half-conscious of himself when creating. He does not know exactly who he is. He learns to know himself only through his creation, in it, and after it. Dostoevsky never set out to find himself; he gave himself without stint in his works. He lost himself in each of the characters of his books, and, for this reason, it is in them that he can be found again. Presently we shall see how painfully awkward he is when speaking in his own name, how eloquent, on the other hand, when his own ideas are expressed by those whom he inspires. It is in endowing them with life that he finds himself. He lives in each of them, and the most obvious result of merging himself in their diversity is the masking of his own inconsistencies.

I know no writer richer in contradictions and inconsistencies than Dostoevsky: Nietzsche would describe them as *antagonisms*. Had he been philosopher instead of novelist, he would certainly have attempted to bring his ideas into line, whereby we should have lost the most precious of them.

The happenings in Dostoevsky's life, however tragic, are but surface disturbances. The passions overwhelming him seem to shake him to the depths; but beyond, there remains an inner chamber, unreached by outside happenings or by passion. In this connection a few of his own words will seem a revelation, if read in conjunction with another passage:

"Without some goal and some effort to reach it, no man can live. When he has lost all hope, all object in life, man often becomes a monster in his misery."[1]

But then he seems still in error where his real goal is concerned, for he adds immediately after: "The one object of the prisoners was freedom and to get out of prison."

These words were written in 1861. Such then was his idea of an aim in life. Of course he was suffering in that dread captivity! (He spent ten years in Siberia: four in prison, then six more in forced military service.) He was suffering; but once more a free man, he could realize that the real goal, the freedom he really longed for, was something deeper and had no connection with the throwing wide of prison gates. In 1874 he could write this extraordinary

[1] *The House of the Dead*, p. 240.

sentence, which I like to compare with what I read to you a moment ago:

"No aim can possibly be worth a wrecked existence."[1]

So, according to Dostoevsky, we have each our reason for living, superior, hidden—hidden often from ourselves—certainly far different from the ostensible goal assigned by most of us to our existence.

Let us first of all try to picture Fyodor Michailovitch Dostoevsky. His friend Riesenkampf delineates him as he was at twenty years of age, in 1841:

"The face was rounded and full; the nose slightly retroussé; the hair light brown, worn short. A broad forehead, and beneath thin eyebrows, little grey eyes, set deep in the head. Pale cheeks, covered with freckles. A sickly, almost livid complexion, and very thick lips."

It is sometimes asserted that his first epileptic attacks occurred in Siberia; but he was a sick man even before sentence was passed on him, and the disease certainly made progress in Siberia. "A sickly complexion." Dostoevsky had always had poor health. And yet he, weak and complaining, was singled out for military service while his robust brother was exempted.

In 1841, that is, at twenty years of age, he was promoted non-commissioned officer, and then, in 1842, he took the examinations and was commissioned ensign. We learn that his officer's pay amounted to 3,000 roubles, and although he had come into his share of the father's fortune after the latter's death, he led a free life, and had to take a younger brother in charge, consequently he was always falling into debt. This money question turns up again and again in his letters, much more urgently than in Balzac's. It plays an extremely important part almost to the very end of his life,

---

[1] Bienstock, p. 449. Letter to Mlle Guérassimov, Petersburg, March 7, 1877.

and it was not until the closing years that he was really freed from his financial worries.

In his young days Dostoevsky indulged in every dissipation. He was assiduous at the play, at concerts, at the ballet. Not a care in the world! He chooses to rent a flat simply because he has taken a fancy to the landlord's appearance. His servant robs him, and he finds entertainment in watching the pilfering continue. His mood changes abruptly, according as fortune smiles or frowns. Faced with his utter inability to steer a course in life, his family and friends are anxious to see him share quarters with Riesenkampf. "Take this real methodical German as your model," they tell him. Riesenkampf, slightly older than Dostoevsky, was a physician, and came to settle down in Petersburg in the year 1843. At this moment, Dostoevsky has not a penny to his name. He is living on bread and milk—both unpaid for. "Fyodor is one of these people in whose company a man lives well, but who himself will remain a needy creature till the very end of his days." They set up quarters together, but Dostoevsky proves himself impossible as a companion. He receives Riesenkampf's patients in the waiting-room, and each time one of them appears needy, Dostoevsky succours him with Riesenkampf's funds or with his own, when he *has* any. One fine day he receives a thousand roubles from Moscow, the bulk of which sum is immediately employed in settling some debts; then, the very same evening, Dostoevsky gambles away the rest, at billiards, by his own account, and the following morning is obliged to borrow five roubles from his friend. I forgot to tell you that the last fifty roubles had been stolen by a patient of Riesenkampf's, whom Dostoevsky, in a sudden manifestation of friendliness, had shown into his room. Riesenkampf and Dostoevsky parted in March, 1844, without much apparent improvement in the latter's ways.

In 1846, he published *Poor Folk*. This book had sudden and considerable success. Dostoevsky's manner of speaking about his success is significant of the man. We read in a contemporary letter:

"It dazes me: I am not living. I haven't time to think. . . . A precarious reputation has been built up around me, and I don't know how long the damnable thing will last."[1]

In 1849, along with a group of suspects, he is taken by the police. This is the affair known as the Petrachevsky Plot.

It is difficult to say what exactly were at this time Dostoevsky's political and social opinions. From this frequenting of suspected individuals we are to infer a great measure of intellectual curiosity and a certain generous warm-heartedness which ran him into unconsidered risks. But we have no authority for believing that Dostoevsky ever was what can be termed an anarchist, a being threatening the safety of the State.

Numerous passages in his letters and in the *Journal of an Author* show him as entertaining quite the opposite ideas, and the whole of *The Possessed* is, as it were, a speech for the prosecution against anarchism. At any rate, taken he was amongst these suspects meeting round Petrachevsky. He was thrown into prison, sent to trial, and heard himself condemned to death. It was only at the eleventh hour that the death sentence was commuted and he was exiled to Siberia. All this is already familiar to you. In these causeries I should like to speak only of what you could not find elsewhere; but, for the sake of such as are unfamiliar with them, I shall read to you some passages from his letters dealing with his sentence and his life in the penal settlement. I consider them very self-revealing. In them we shall see, through

[1] Bienstock, p. 94. Letter to his brother Michael, spring of 1847.

the portrayal of his sufferings, appear again and again the optimism that supported him all his days. This is what he wrote on July 18, 1849, from the fortress where he lay awaiting the verdict.

"Human beings have an incredible amount of endurance and will to live; I should never have expected to find so much in myself; now I know from experience that it is there."[1]

Then in August, weighed down by ill-health:

"To lose courage is to sin . . . work, ever more work, *con amore*, therein lies real happiness."[2]

And again, on September 14, 1849:

"I had expected worse. And I know now that I have in me such reserves of vitality that it would be difficult to exhaust."[3]

I shall read almost the whole of his short letter dated December 22.

"To-day, December 22, we were led out to Semionovsky Square. There the death warrant was read over to us all, we were given the cross to kiss, swords were snapped above our heads, and our last toilet was performed (white shirts). Then, three of us were placed against posts for execution. I was the sixth; we were called up in threes, so I came in the second group, and I had a few moments left to live. I thought of you, brother, and of yours; at that last moment you alone were in my thoughts, and then I realized how much I loved you, beloved brother! I had time to kiss Plestcheyev and Dourov, who were beside me, and bid them farewell. At last the retreat was sounded, those tied to the

[1] Bienstock, p. 98. Letter to his brother Michael, from the fortress, July 18, 1849.

[2] *Ibid.*, p. 100. Letter to his brother Michael, from the fortress, August 27, 1849.

[3] *Ibid.*, p. 101. Letter to his brother Michael, from the fortress, September 14, 1849.

posts were fetched back, and it was read out to us that His
Imperial Majesty was pleased to spare our lives."[1]

In Dostoevsky's novels we shall come across again and
again more or less direct allusions to the death sentence and
to the condemned man's last hours. I cannot dwell on this
for the moment.

Before starting out for Semipalatinsk, he was granted half
an hour to take leave of his brother Michael. Of the two, he
was the calmer, a friend relates, and said:

"In the settlement, dear brother, the convicts are not wild
beasts, just men, better men than I perhaps, more deserving,
too, maybe. Yes, we shall meet again, I hope: I am sure we
shall see each other again. Only do write to me and send me
books. I shall soon let you know which to send: surely
reading is permitted there." (This, says the narrator, was a
white lie to comfort his brother.) "As soon as I am released,
I shall begin to write. I have *lived* during these last months,
and in the days before me, what shall I not see and live
through? After all that I shall not lack material for writing."[2]

During the four years of Siberia which followed,
Dostoevsky was not permitted to write to his family.
At any rate the existing volume of correspondence contains
no letters from this period, nor do Orest Müller's *Documents*
(*Materialen*), published in 1883, indicate any. But since the
issue of these *Documents* numerous Dostoevsky letters have
been found and published; doubtless still more will yet be
discovered.

According to Müller, Dostoevsky left the penal settlement
on March 2, 1854: according to official records, on January
23. These same archives mention nineteen letters written by
Fyodor Dostoevsky between March 16, 1854 and September

---

1 Bienstock, p. 103. Letter to his brother Michael, from the fortress,
December 22, 1849.

2 A. P. Miliukov in his *Reminiscences*, 1881.

11, 1856 to his brother, relatives, and friends during the years of military service at Semipalatinsk, where his sentence was completed. The French translation gives only twelve of these letters, omitting (and why I cannot tell) that admirable letter dated February 22, 1854, which, originally translated and printed in Numbers 12 and 13 of *La Vogue*, 1886, now only with difficulty accessible, was reprinted in the February issue of the *Nouvelle Revue Française*, 1922.

Seeing this letter is not to be found in the published volume of Dostoevsky's correspondence, allow me to read some lengthy extracts from it:[1]

(February 22, 1854.) "At last I can talk with you somewhat more explicitly, and, I believe, in a more reasonable manner. But before I write another line I *must* ask you: tell me, for God's sake, why you have never written me a single syllable till now? Could I have expected this from you? Believe me, in my lonely and isolated state, I sometimes fell into utter despair, for I believed that you were no longer alive; through whole nights I would brood upon what was to become of your children, and I cursed my fate because I could not help them. . . ."

You see his keenest suffering is not in the consciousness of his own abandonment, but in the realization of his powerlessness to help.

"How can I impart to you what is now in my mind—the things I thought, the things I did, the convictions I acquired, the conclusions I came to? I cannot even attempt the task. It is absolutely impossible. I don't like to leave a piece of work half done; to say only a part is to say nothing. At any rate, you now have my detailed report in your hands: read it, and get from it what you will. It is my duty to tell you all, and so I will begin with my recollections. Do you remember how we parted from each other, dear beloved fellow? You had

[1] See Mayne, pp. 51 sqq.

scarcely left me when we three, Dourov, Yastryembsky, and
I, were led out to have the irons put on. Precisely at midnight on that Christmas Eve (1849) did chains touch me for
the first time. They weigh about ten pounds, and make
walking extraordinarily difficult. Then we were sent into
open sledges, each with a gendarme; and so, in four sledges,
the orderly opening the procession, we left Petersburg.
I was heavy-hearted, and the many different impressions
filled me with confused and uncertain sensations. My
heart beat with a peculiar flutter, and that numbed its
pain. Still, the fresh air was reviving in its effect, and, since it
is usual before all new experiences to be aware of a curious
vivacity and eagerness, so I was at the bottom quite tranquil.
I looked attentively at all the festively-lit houses of Petersburg, and said good-bye to each. They drove us past your
abode, and at Krayevsky's the windows were brilliantly lit.
You had told me he was giving a Christmas party and tree,
and that your children were going to it, with Emilie
Fyodorovna; I did feel dreadfully sad as we passed that
house. I took leave, as it were, of the little ones. I felt so
lonely for them, and even years afterwards I often thought
of them with tears in my eyes. We were driven beyond
Yaroslavl; after three or four stations we stopped, in the first
grey of morning, at Schlüsselburg, and went into an inn.
There we drank tea with as much avidity as if we had not
touched anything for a week. After the eight months'
captivity, sixty versts in a sledge gave us appetites of which,
even to-day, I think with pleasure.

"I was in a good temper. Dourov chattered incessantly,
and Yastryembsky expressed unwonted apprehensions for
the future. We all laid ourselves out to become better
acquainted with our orderly. He was a good old man, very
friendlily inclined towards us: a man who had seen a lot of
life; he had travelled all over Europe with dispatches. On the

way he showed us many kindnesses. His name was Kusma Prokofyevitch Prokofyev. Among other things he let us have a covered sledge, which was very welcome, for the frost was fearful.

"The second day was a holiday; the drivers, who were changed at the various stations, wore cloaks of grey German cloth and bright red belts; in the village streets there was not a soul to be seen. It was a splendid winter day. They drove us through the remote parts of the Petersburg, Novgorod, and Yaroslavl Governments. There were quite insignificant little towns, at great distances from one another. But as we were passing through on a holiday, there was always plenty to eat and drink; we drove—drove terribly. We were warmly dressed, it is true, but we had to sit for ten hours at a time in the sledges, halting at only five or six stations; it was almost unendurable. I froze to the marrow, and could scarcely thaw myself in the warm rooms at the stations. Strange to say, the journey completely restored me to health. Near Perm, we had a frost of 40 degrees during some of the nights. I don't recommend that to you. It was highly disagreeable.

"Mournful was the moment when we crossed the Urals. The horses and sledges sank deep in the snow; a snowstorm was raging. We got out of the sledge—it was night—and waited, standing, till they were extricated. All about us whirled the snowstorm. We were standing on the confines of Europe and Asia; before us lay Siberia and the mysterious future—behind us, our whole past; it was very melancholy. Tears came to my eyes. On the way, the peasants would stream out of all the villages to see us; and although we were fettered, prices were trebled to us at all the stations. Kusma Prokofyevitch took half our expenses on himself, though we tried hard to prevent him; in this way each of us, during the whole journey, spent only fifteen roubles.

"On January 12, 1850, we came to Tobolsk. After we had been paraded before the authorities, and searched, in which proceeding all our money was taken from us, myself, Dourov and Yastryembsky were taken into one cell; the others, Spejechynov, etc., who had arrived before us, were in another section, and during the whole time we hardly once saw each other. I should like to tell you more of our six days' stay in Tobolsk, and of the impression it made upon me. But I haven't room here. I will only tell you that the great compassion and sympathy which was shown to us there, made up to us, like a big piece of happiness, for all that had gone before. The prisoners of former days[1] (and still more their wives) cared for us as if they had been our kith and kin. Those noble souls, tested by five-and-twenty years of suffering and self-sacrifice! We saw them but seldom, for we were very rigidly guarded; still they sent us clothes and provisions, they comforted and encouraged us. I had brought far too few clothes, and had bitterly repented it; but they sent me clothes. Finally we left Tobolsk, and reached Omsk in three days.

"While I was in Tobolsk, I gathered information about my future superiors. They told me that the Commandant was a very decent fellow, but that the Major, Krivzov, was an uncommon brute, a petty tyrant, a drunkard, a trickster—in short, the greatest horror that can be imagined. From the very beginning, he called both Dourov and me blockhead, and vowed to chastise us bodily at the first transgression. He had already held his position for two years, and done the most hideous and unsanctioned things; two years later he was court-martialled for them. So God protected me from him! He used to come to us mad drunk (I never once saw him sober), and would seek out some inoffensive person and flog him on the pretext that he—the prisoner—was drunk.

[1] The *Decembrists*.

Often he came at night and punished at random—say, because such and such a one was sleeping on his left side instead of his right, or because he talked or moaned in his sleep—in fact, anything that occurred to his drunken mind. I should have had to break out in the long run against such a man as that, and it was he who wrote the monthly reports of us to Petersburg.

"I spent the whole four years behind dungeon walls, and only left the prison when I was taken on 'hard labour'. The work was hard, though not always; sometimes in bad weather, in rain, or in winter during the unendurable frosts, my strength would forsake me. Once I had to spend four hours at a piece of extra work, and in such frost that the quicksilver froze; it was perhaps 40 degrees below zero. One of my feet was frost-bitten. We all lived together in one barrack-room. Imagine an old, crazy, wooden building, that should long ago have been broken up as useless. In the summer it is unbearably hot, in the winter unbearably cold. All the boards are rotten; on the ground filth lies an inch thick; every instant one is in danger of slipping and coming down. The small windows are so frozen over that even by day one can hardly read. The ice on the panes is three inches thick. The ceilings drip, there are draughts everywhere. We are packed like herrings in a barrel. The stove is heated with six logs of wood, but the room is so cold that the ice never thaws; the atmosphere is unbearable—and so through all the winter long.

"In the same room, the prisoners wash their linen, and thus make the place so wet that one scarcely dares to move. From twilight till morning we are forbidden to leave the barrack-room; the doors are barricaded; in the ante-room a great wooden trough for the calls of nature is placed; this makes one almost unable to breathe. All the prisoners stink like pigs; they say that they can't help it, for they must live, and are but men. We sleep upon bare boards; each man was allowed one pillow only. We covered ourselves with short sheepskins, and our feet were outside the covering all the time. It was thus that we froze night after night. Fleas, lice, and other vermin by the bushel. In the winter we got thin sheepskins to wear, which didn't keep us warm at all, and boots with short legs; thus equipped, we had to go out into the frost.

"To eat we got bread and cabbage soup; the soup should, by the regulations, have contained a quarter pound of meat per head; but they put in sausage-meat, and so I never came across a piece of genuine flesh. On feast days we got porridge, but with scarcely any butter. On fast days, cabbage and nothing else. My stomach went utterly to pieces, and I suffered tortures from indigestion.

"From all this you can see yourself that one couldn't live there at all without money; if I had had none, I should most assuredly have perished; no one could endure such a life. But every convict does some sort of work and sells it, thus earning, every single one of them, a few pence. I often drank tea and bought myself a piece of meat; it was my salvation. It was quite impossible to do without smoking, for otherwise the stench would have choked one. All these things were done behind the backs of the officials.

"I was often in hospital. My nerves were so shattered that I had some epileptic fits—however, that was not often. I have rheumatism in my legs now, too. But except for that, I feel right well. Add to all these discomforts the fact that it was almost impossible to get one's self a book, and that when I did get one, I had to read it on the sly; that all around me was incessant malignity, turbulence, and quarrelling; then perpetual espionage, and the impossibility *of ever being alone*, even for an instant—and so without variation for four long years. You'll believe me when I tell you I was not happy! And imagine, in addition, the ever-present dread of drawing down some punishment on myself, the irons, and the utter oppression of spirits—and you have the picture of my life.

"I won't even try to tell you what transformations were undergone by my soul, my faith, my mind, and my heart, in those four years. It would be a long story. Still, the eternal concentration, the escape into myself from bitter reality, did bear its fruit. I now have many new needs and hopes of which I never thought in other days. But all this will be pure enigma for you, so I'll pass to other things. I will say only one word: do not forget me, and do help me! I need books and money. Send them me, for Christ's sake.

"Omsk is a hateful hole. There is hardly a tree there. In summer, heat and winds that bring sandstorms; in winter, snowstorms. I have scarcely seen anything of the country around. The place is dirty, almost exclusively inhabited by military, and dissolute to the last degree. I mean the common people. If I hadn't discovered some human beings here, I should have gone utterly to the dogs.

"Constantine Ivanovitch Ivanov is like a brother to me. He has done everything that he in any way could for me. I owe him money. If he ever goes to Petersburg, show him some recognition. I owe him twenty-five roubles. But how can I repay his kindness, his constant willingness to carry out all my requests, his attention and care for me, just like a brother's? And he is not the only one I have to thank in that way. *Brother, there are very many noble natures in the world.*

"I have already said that your silence often tortures me. I thank you for the money you sent. In your next letter (even if it's '*official*,' for I don't know yet whether it is possible for me to correspond with you)—in your next, write as fully as you can of all your affairs, of Emilie Fyodorovna, the children, all relations and acquaintances; also of those in Moscow—who is alive and who is dead; and of your business; tell me what capital you started with, whether it is lucrative, whether you are in funds, finally, whether you will help me financially, and how much you will send me a year. But send no money with the official letter—particularly if I don't find a covering address. For the present, give Michael Petrovitch as the consignor of all packets (you understand, don't you?). For the time, I have some money, but I have no books. If you can, send me the magazines for this year, or at any rate the O.Z. (*Annals of the Homeland*).

"But what I urgently need are the following: I need (very necessary!) ancient historians (in French translation), modern historians: Guizot, Thierry, Thiers, Ranke, and so forth; national studies, and the Fathers of the Church. Choose the cheapest and most compact editions. Send them by return.

"People try to console me: 'They're quite simple sort of fellows there.' But I dread simple men more than complex ones. For that matter, men everywhere are just—men. Even among the robber-murderers in the prison, I came to know some men in those four years. Believe me, there were among them deep, strong, beautiful natures, and it often gave me great joy to find gold under a rough exterior. And not in a single case, or even two, but in several cases. Some inspired respect, others were downright fine. I taught the Russian language to a young Circassian—he had been transported to Siberia for robbery with murder. How grateful he was to me! Another convict wept when I said good-bye to him. Certainly I had often given him money, but it was so little, and his gratitude so boundless! My character, though, was deteriorating; in my relations with others I was ill-tempered and impatient. They accounted for it by my mental condition, and bore all without grumbling.

A propos, what a number of national types and characters I became familiar with in prison! I lived *into* their lives, and so I believe I know them really well. Many tramps' and thieves' careers were laid bare to me, and above all, the whole wretched existence of the common people. Decidedly I have not spent my time there in vain. I have learnt to know the Russian people as only a few know them. I am a little vain of it. I hope that such vanity is pardonable. . . .

"Send me the Koran, and Kant's *Critique of Pure Reason*, and if you have the chance of sending me anything not officially, then be sure to send Hegel, but particularly Hegel's *History of Philosophy*. Upon that depends my whole future. For God's sake, exert yourself to get me transferred to the Caucasus; try to find out from well-informed sources whether I shall be permitted to print my works, and in what way I should seek this sanction. I intend to try for permission in two or three years. I beg you to sustain me so long. Without money I shall be destroyed by military life. So please! . . .

"Now I mean to write novels and plays. But I must still read a great deal. Don't forget me.

"Once again farewell.

"F. D."[1]

This letter, like so many others, remained unanswered. It is evident that Dostoevsky was left without news from his family during his whole term of imprisonment. Are we to suppose, on his brother's part, prudence, fear of compromising himself, or maybe indifference? I cannot tell. Mme Hoffmann, in her biography, inclines to the last-mentioned supposition.

The first we know of Dostoevsky's letters subsequent to

[1] Mayne, pp. 51–65.

his release and enlistment in the 7th Siberian Line Regiment is dated March 27, 1854. It does not appear in the French edition of his correspondence. In this letter we read as follows:

"Send me—not newspapers, but European histories. Economists—Church Fathers—as many of the classics as possible. Herodotus, Thucydides, Tacitus, Pliny, Flavius, Plutarch, Diodorus, etc., in French translations. And the Koran and a German Dictionary. Not all at once, of course, but as much as you can. Send me Pissaren's *Physics* too, and a manual of physiology, any one, in French if better than in Russian. All in the cheapest editions. Not in one consignment, but slowly, one book after another. I shall be grateful for every little thing you can do for me. Do realize how urgently I need this intellectual food! . . ."

"Now you know my chief occupations," he writes a little later. "Really I have none but these connected with my duty. No outside events, no disturbances in my life, no mishaps. But what is happening in soul, heart, and mind, what has sprung up, ripened or been blighted, what has been cast aside with the tares, *that* cannot be told and written down on a scrap of paper. Here I live in isolation; I shrink out of sight, as usual. Moreover, for five years I lived with an escort, and there are times when it is pure bliss for me to be alone. On the whole, prison has destroyed many things in me and created new. For example, I've already spoken about my illness: strange attacks resembling epilepsy. And yet not epilepsy. Some day I shall give you particulars."[1]

In the last of these causeries we shall come back to this terrible question of his illness.

In a letter dated November 6 of the same year we find:

[1] Bienstock, pp. 104-5. Letter to his brother Michael, Semipalatinsk, July 30, 1854.

"It will soon be ten months since I took up my new life. As for the other four years, I look upon them as a period when I was buried alive and closed in a coffin. What terrible years! I cannot, my friend, tell you how terrible. Unspeakable suffering without end, for every hour, every minute lay heavy on my soul. During the whole of these four years, not a moment but what I was conscious of my prison walls."[1]

But, immediately after, watch how far his optimism rises above it all:

"I was so busy all summer that I had scarcely time for sleep. But now I have grown used to things. My health too has improved slightly. And hope not wholly lost, I can look at the future with moderate fortitude."[2]

Three letters from the same period were given in the *Niva*, April, 1898. Of these the French edition of Dostoevsky's *Correspondence* includes the first only. In one (August 21, 1855) there is reference to a letter of the previous October, which has not been traced.

"When, in my letter of last October, I repeated my complaints at your silence, you answered that these had made very painful reading for you. Oh, Mysha! for the love of God, bear me no ill-will; remember my loneliness. I am like a pebble cast aside. I've always been of a gloomy, sickly, susceptible disposition. I am myself thoroughly convinced I was in the wrong."

Dostoevsky returned to Petersburg on November 29, 1859. At Semipalatinsk he had married the widow of a deportee, mother of a growing son whose intelligence seemingly was less than mediocre. Dostoevsky adopted the

---

[1] Bienstock, p. 106. Letter to his brother Andrey, Semipalatinsk, November 6, 1854.

[2] *Ibid.*, p. 107. Letter to his brother Andrey, Semipalatinsk, November 6, 1854.

boy, for whom he made himself answerable. He had a perfect mania for assuming burdens.

"He was but little altered," his friend Miliukov tells us. "His mien is more confident than of yore, and his features have lost none of the energy they used to express."

In 1861 he published *The Insulted and Injured*; in 1861–2 his *Memories of the House of the Dead*. *Crime and Punishment*, the first of his great novels, did not appear till 1866.

During the years 1863–1865, he busied himself actively with a review. One of his letters speaks so eloquently of the years between that I must read further passages: this is, I think, the last time I shall quote to you from his correspondence! This particular letter is dated March 31, 1865.

"I am going to recount my life during this time. Not the whole of it, though. That is impossible, for in such a case one never tells in letters the essential facts. There are things I cannot narrate simply. That's why I shall confine myself to a summary account of the past year of my life.

"You probably know that four years ago my brother Michael undertook the publication of a review, wherein I collaborated. Everything was going well. My *House of the Dead* had met with considerable success and given a fresh lease of life to my literary reputation. When my brother began publication, he owed a lot of money; his debts were being paid off when suddenly, in May, 1863, the review was suspended on account of a strong and patriotic article, which, misinterpreted, was read as a protest against the conduct of the Government and public opinion. The blow killed him; debt after debt accumulated, and his health became impaired. At the moment, I was far away, in Moscow, at the bedside of my dying wife. Yes, dear friend, you wrote to sympathize in my cruel loss, the death of my beloved brother, but you did not know how heavy the hand of fate was upon me. Another creature who loved me, and whom I loved infinitely—my wife—died of consumption in Moscow, where she had been settled for a twelve-month. The whole winter of 1864 I never left her bedside. . . .

". . . Ah, dear friend, she loved me deeply, and I returned her love; yet, we did not live happily together. I shall tell you all about it when I see you. Let me say just this. Although we were unhappy (by reason of her difficult character—she was hypochondriac, and full of a sick woman's whims), we could not cease to love each other. Indeed, the unhappier we grew, the closer we were drawn together. Strange though it may seem, it is true. She was the best, the noblest, the most generous-hearted woman I have ever known. After she was gone (despite all my anxieties during the twelve-month I watched her dying), although I felt and painfully realized what I was burying with her, I could not picture the emptiness and misery of my life. That is a year ago now, and the feeling is still the same.

"Immediately after the funeral, I hastened to Petersburg and to my brother. He alone was left me! Three months later he, too, was no more. His illness lasted only a month. It did not appear serious and the attack which carried him off in three days was practically unforeseen.

"Then I was suddenly left alone; and I knew fear! It has become terrible! My life is broken in two. On one hand, the past, with all that I had to live for; on the other, the unknown, with not one loving heart to comfort me in my loss. There was literally no reason why I should go on living. Forge new links, start a fresh existence? The very thought revolted me! Then I realized for the first time that I could not replace my loved ones; they were all I held dear, and new loves could not, ought not to exist."[1]

[1] Bienstock, pp. 233–5. Letter to Baron Alexander Wrangel, Petersburg, March 31, 1865.

This letter was continued in April, and a fortnight after this cry of despair, we read, under the date April 14: "Of all my reserves of strength and energy, there is nothing left save a vague uneasiness of soul, a state bordering on despair. Bitterness and indecision—a mood foreign to me. And then I'm utterly alone. I've lost the friend of a lifetime. Yet I always have the feeling that I am going to begin to live! Ridiculous, isn't it? The cat and its nine lives?"[1]

He adds these words: "I write to you at great length, and I see that of the very essence of my moral or spiritual life I have given you not a notion," which passage I should like to set side by side with an extraordinary paragraph I find in *Crime and Punishment*.

In this novel Dostoevsky tells us the story of Raskolnikov, who commits a crime and is sent to Siberia. In the last pages he speaks of the strange feeling that takes possession of his hero's being, the feeling that at last he is going to live. "And what were all, all the agonies of the past! Everything, even his crime, sentence, and imprisonment, seemed to him now in the first rush of feeling an external, strange fact, with which he had no concern. But he could not think for long together of anything that evening, and he could not have analysed consciously, he was simply feeling. Life had stepped into the place of theory."[2]

These sentences I have read to you in justification of my opening remarks. The great external events of Dostoevsky's life, tragic though they were, are less important than this one small fact which it is now time to consider. During his years in Siberia, Dostoevsky made the acquaintance of a woman who put the New Testament into his hand—this, by the way, being the only officially sanctioned reading matter in gaol.

[1] Bienstock, p. 239. Letter to Baron Alexander Wrangel, Petersburg. April 14, 1865.

[2] *Crime and Punishment*, p. 492.

This reading and meditating the Gospels was of vital importance to Dostoevsky. All his subsequently written works are steeped in the teaching of the Gospels, and we shall be obliged again and again to revert to the truths he discovered in reading them.

I find it highly interesting to observe and compare in two natures akin in so many respects, Nietzsche and Dostoevsky, the very different reactions to contact with the Gospels. With Nietzsche the reaction, immediate and marked, was, we may as well admit, jealousy. It does not seem to me possible to understand Nietzsche's works without taking account of this feeling. Nietzsche was jealous of Jesus Christ, jealous to the point of madness. In writing his *Zarathustra*, Nietzsche is ever harassed by his desire to write a counterpart to the Gospels. He even adopts at times the form of the Beatitudes the better to make mockery of them. He wrote the *Anti-Christ*, and in his last work, *Ecce Homo*, he poses as the adversary triumphant of Him he sought to oust.

With Dostoevsky the reaction is far different. He felt at once that he was face to face with something superior, not only to himself, but to entire mankind, something divine. ... The humility of which I spoke earlier in the day, and to which I shall time and again return, predisposed him to making submission before what was avowedly better and higher than himself. He bowed his head humbly before Jesus Christ, and the first, the greatest consequence of his submission and self-surrender was the safeguarding intact his nature's rich complexity. No artist ever more truly practised the teaching of the Gospel: *"For whosoever will save his life shall lose it; but whosoever will lose his life for My sake, the same shall save it."*

By reason of this sacrifice and renunciation the most discordant elements are able to live side by side in Dostoevsky's soul, and the extraordinary wealth of antagonisms is preserved.

At our next meeting we shall inquire whether several of Dostoevsky's characteristics, which to us Westerners seem perchance more than strange, are not common to all Russians, and by so inquiring we may be enabled to discern such features as are more purely individual and personal.

II

THE few psychological and moral truths Dostoevsky's works will permit us to touch upon are in my estimation so important that I am all eagerness to reach them. By their very boldness and originality they would seem paradoxical to you if I approached them directly. I needs must proceed warily.

In our last talk I spoke to you of the figure of the man himself. The moment is favourable, I think, for presenting it in its own atmosphere the better to bring its particular features into relief.

I have been on intimate terms with some Russians, but I have never been in Russia; hence, without help, my task would be extremely difficult. I shall first of all submit a few observations on the Russian people that I found in a German monograph on Dostoevsky. Mme Hoffmann, in her excellent biography, insists first and foremost on the solidarity, the common brotherhood between all classes of Russian society, which end in sweeping away social barriers and facilitate naturally the freedom of intercourse we find in all Dostoevsky's novels. An introduction, a sudden feeling of sympathetic understanding; and we have at once what one of his heroes so expressively describes as "chance relationships." Homes are transformed into hostelries, the stranger of yesterday becomes the honoured guest of to-day: a friend's friend visits you, and immediately everything between you is on a footing of intimacy.

Another observation of Mme Hoffmann's concerning the Russian people. It is inherently incapable of leading a strict and methodical existence, of being punctual even. It

would seem as if the Russian did not suffer much in consequence of his own improvidence, for he makes no great
effort to free himself from it. And if I may be permitted to
seek an excuse for the lack of order in my causeries, I shall
find it in the very confusion of Dostoevsky's ideas, in their
extreme entanglement and in the peculiar difficulties experi-
enced in trying to hold them to a plan which satisfies our
Western logic. This wavering and indecision Mme
Hoffmann ascribes partly to the weakening of time sense
due to the endless summer days and interminable winter
nights, when the rhythm of the passing hours is lost.
In a short address delivered at the *Vieux Colombier* I already
quoted Mme Hoffmann's illustration of the Russian who
met reproaches on account of his unpunctuality with
"Yes, life is difficult! There are moments which must be
lived well, and this is more important than the punctual
keeping of any engagement!"—a sentence full of singifi-
cance, for it reveals at the same time the strange consciousness a Russian has of his inner life, more important to him
than all social connections.

I should like to point out, with Mme Hoffmann, the
propensity to pity and suffering, *Leiden und Mitleiden*, to
compassion extending even to the criminal. In Russia there
exists but one word to designate the poor and the criminal,
but one to cover actual crime and ordinary offences. Add to
this an almost religious contrition and we shall the better
understand the Russian's ineradicable mistrustfulness in all
his relations with strangers, with foreigners in particular.
Westerners often complain of this mistrustfulness, which
proceeds, so Mme Hoffmann maintains, from the uneasy
consciousness of his own insufficiency and proneness to sin,
rather than from any feeling that other people are of no
account: it is a mistrust that springs from humility of spirit.

Nothing could better throw light on this strange

religiosity of the Russian, which persists even when belief is long since dead, than the four conversations of Prince Myshkin, the hero of *The Idiot*. These I shall now read to you.

"'As to the question of faith,' he began, smiling, . . . 'I had four different conversations in two days last week. I came in the morning by the new railway and talked for four hours with a man in the train. We made friends on the spot. I had heard a great deal about him beforehand and had heard he was an atheist, among other things. He really is a very learned man. What's more, he's an unusually well-bred man, so that he talked to me quite as if I were his equal in ideas and attainments. He doesn't believe in God. Only, one thing struck me: that he seemed not to be talking about that at all the whole time; and it struck me, just because whenever I have met unbelievers before, or read their books, it always seemed to me that they were speaking and writing in their books about something quite different, although it seemed to me about that on the surface. I said so to him at the time, but I suppose I didn't say so clearly, or did not know how to express it, for he didn't understand. In the evening, I stopped for the night at a provincial hotel, and a murder had just been committed there the night before, so that every one was talking about it when I arrived. Two peasants, middle-aged men, friends who had known each other for a long time, and were not drunk, had had tea and were meaning to go to bed in the same room. But one had noticed during those last two days that the other was wearing a silver watch on a yellow bead chain, which he seems not to have seen on him before. The man was not a thief: he was an honest man, in fact, and by a peasant's standard by no means poor. But he was so taken by the watch, and so fascinated by it, that at last he could not restrain himself. He took a knife and when his friend had turned away, he approached him cautiously from behind, and praying fervently, "God forgive me for Christ's sake!" he cut his friend's throat at one stroke like a sheep and took his watch.'

"Rogozhin went off into peals of laughter; he laughed as though he were in a sort of fit. It was positively strange to see such laughter after the gloomy mood that had preceded it.

" 'I do like that! Yes, that beats everything!' he cried convulsively, gasping for breath. 'One man doesn't believe in God at all, while the other believes in him so thoroughly that he prays as he murders men! . . . You could never have invented that, brother! Ha!—ha!—ha! That beats everything!'

" 'Next morning I went out to walk about the town,' Myshkin went on, as soon as Rogozhin was quiet again, though his lips still quivered with spasmodic convulsive laughter. 'I saw a drunken soldier in a terribly disorderly state staggering about the wooden pavement. He came up to me. "Buy a silver cross, sir!" said he. "I'll let you have it for twenty kopecks. It's silver." I saw in his hand a cross—he must have just taken it off—on a very dirty blue ribbon; but one could see at once it was only tin. It was a big one with eight corners, of a regular Byzantine pattern. I took out twenty kopecks and gave them to him, and at once put the cross round my neck; and I could see from his face how glad he was that he had cheated a stupid gentleman, and he went off immediately to drink what he had got for it, there was no doubt about that. At that time, brother, I was quite carried away by the rush of impressions that burst upon me in Russia; I had understood nothing about Russia before. I had grown up, as it were, inarticulate, and my memories of my country were somehow fantastic during those five years abroad. Well, I walked on, thinking, "Yes, I'll put off judging that man who sold his Christ. God only knows what's hidden in these weak drunken beasts." An hour later, when

I was going back to the hotel, I came upon a peasant woman with a tiny baby in her arms. She was quite a young woman, and the baby was about six weeks old. The baby smiled at her for the first time in its life. "What are you doing, my dear?" (I was always asking questions in those days.) "God has just such gladness every time He sees from heaven that a sinner is praying to him with all his heart, as a mother has when she sees the first smile on her baby's face." That was what the woman said to me almost in those words, this deep, subtle, and truly religious thought—a thought in which all the essence of Christianity finds expression; that is the whole conception of God as our Father and of God's gladness in man, like a father's in his own child—the fundamental idea of Christ! A simple peasant woman! It's true she was a mother . . . and who knows, very likely that woman was the wife of that soldier. Listen, Parfyon! You asked me a question just now; here is my answer. The essence of religious feeling does not come under any sort of reasoning or atheism, and has nothing to do with any crimes or misdemeanours. There is something else here, and there will always be something else—something that the atheists will for ever slur over; they will always be talking of something else. But the chief thing is that you will notice it more clearly and quickly in the Russian heart than anywhere else. And this is my conclusion. It's one of the chief convictions I've gathered from our Russia. There is work to be done, Parfyon! There is work to be done in our Russian world, believe me.' "[1]

And we see at the end of this story another characteristic reveal itself: the belief in the special mission of the Russian people.

This belief we find in several Russian writers: in Dostoevsky it becomes an active and painful conviction, and

[1] *The Idiot*, pp. 217-20.

his chief grievance against Turgeniev was simply that he could not trace in him this national feeling, his opinion being that Turgeniev was too westernized.

In his speech at the Pushkin celebrations, Dostoevsky declared that Pushkin, still in full flush of imitating Byron and Chénier, suddenly found what Dostoevsky calls the "Russian note," a note "fresh and sincere." Replying to the question (which he describes as "accursed") "What faith can we have in the Russian people and in its worth?" Pushkin exclaimed, "Humble thyself, thou son of arrogance, and first conquer thy pride. Humble thyself and before the people, bend thy neck towards thy mother earth."

Never perhaps are ethnic differences more clearly marked than when the manner of interpreting *honour* is involved. The hidden mainspring of civilized man's conduct seems to me to be less a matter of amour-propre, as La Rochefoucauld would have said, than a feeling for what we call the "point of honour." This feeling for personal honour, this sensitive spot, is not exactly alike for Frenchman, Englishman, Italian, and Spaniard. But contrasted with the Russian conception, the codes of honour of all Western nations seem to fuse practically into one. When we appreciate the Russians' idea of honour, we see at once how often the code of the Western world is opposed to the teaching of the Gospels. And the Russian idea of honour is as much closer to the Gospels by virtue of its remoteness from Western nations; in other words, Christian feeling is predominant in the Russians, and often takes precedence of "honour" as we Westerners interpret the idea.

Faced with the choice of seeking revenge or asking pardon by admitting himself in the wrong, the Westerner will often consider the second alternative lacking in dignity, the attitude of a coward or a nonentity. The Westerner tends to esteem unwillingness to forgive, forget, or remit offences a mark of strength of character, and certainly he tries never to put himself in the wrong; but, should he have done so, it would appear that the most unpleasant thing that could befall him would be the necessity for admitting the fact! The Russian, on the other hand, is ever ready to admit himself in the wrong—and even before his enemies—equally willing to humble himself and seek forgiveness.

The Greek Orthodox religion, no doubt, is only encouraging a national inclination by tolerating, nay, approving, public confession. The notion of confession, not murmured low into priestly ears, but made openly, before any and all, comes up again and again, almost with the quality of an obsession, in Dostoevsky's novels. When Raskolnikhov has confessed his crime to Sonia, in *Crime and Punishment*, she advises him, as the one means of unburdening his soul, at once to prostrate himself in the public street and cry aloud, "I have the blood of a fellow-being on my hands." Most of Dostoevsky's characters are seized at certain moments—and almost in invariably unexpected and ill-advised fashion—with the urgent desire to make confession, to ask pardon of some fellow-creature who often has not a notion what it is all about, the desire to place themselves in a posture of inferiority to the person addressed.

You remember, I am sure, the extraordinary scene in *The Idiot*, in the course of an evening party at Nastasya Filippovna's house. To pass the time someone suggested in place of parlour games or charades that each guest should confess the vilest act he ever committed; and the wonderful part is that the suggestion was not scouted, and that each one present commenced his or her confession, with varying degree of sincerity, no doubt, but almost without a vestige of shame.

And more curious still, an anecdote from Dostoevsky's own life, which I have from a Russian in his intimate circle.

I was imprudent enough to tell it to several individuals and already it has been made use of; but in the form I found it retailed, it was fast approaching unrecognizability. Hence my anxiety to give the exact facts here.

There are, in Dostoevsky's life, certain extremely obscure episodes. One, in particular, already alluded to in *Crime and Punishment* and which seems to have served as theme for a certain chapter in *The Possessed*. This chapter does not figure in the novel, having been so far withheld in Russia even. It has, I believe, been printed in Germany, but in an edition for private circulation only.[1] It deals with the rape of a young girl. The child victim hangs herself, and in the next room, Stavrogin, the guilty man, knowing that she is hanging herself waits until life has left her little body. What measure of truth is there in this sinister tale? For the moment, it is not for me to say. The fact remains that Dostoevsky, after an adventure of this nature, was moved to what one must needs describe as remorse. This remorse preyed upon him for a while, and doubtless he said to himself what Sonia said to Raskolnikov. The need for confession became urgent, but confession not merely to a priest. He sought to find the person before whom confession would cause him the acutest suffering. Turgeniev, without the shadow of a doubt! Dostoevsky had not seen him for long, and was on uncommonly bad terms with him. M. Turgeniev was a respectable man, rich, famous, and held in wide esteem. Dostoevsky summoned up all his courage, or rather, he succumbed to a kind of giddiness, to a mysterious and awful attraction. Picture Turgeniev's comfortable study: the author himself at his desk.—The bell rings.—A manservant announces Fyodor Dostoevsky.—What is his business?—He is shown in, and at once begins to tell his tale.—

[1] See *Nouvelle Revue Française*, June–July, 1922, and *Stavrogin's Confession*, translated, with introductory and explanatory notes, by S. S. Koteliansky and *Virginia Woolf*, 1922. (*Translator's note.*)

Turgeniev listens, dumb with stupefaction. What business of his is all this? No doubt the other man is mad!—After the confession, a great silence. Dostoevsky waits for some word or sign from Turgeniev, believing no doubt that like in his own novels, Turgeniev will take him in his arms, kiss him and weep over him, and be reconciled . . . but nothing happens:

"Monsieur Turgeniev, I must tell you how deeply I despise myself. . . ."

He pauses again. . . . The silence remains unbroken until Dostoevsky, unable to contain himself any longer, bursts out in wrath: "But *you* I despise even more! That's all I wanted to say to you," and off he goes, slamming the door behind him.

Here we see how humility is suddenly displaced by a very different feeling. The man who in his humility was abasing himself, draws up in revolt at the humiliation. Humility opens the gates of Heaven: humiliation the gates of Hell. Humility implies a measure of free-will submission; it is accepted without constraint and proves the truth of the Gospel teaching: *"For whosoever exalteth himself shall be abased: and he that humbleth himself shall be exalted."* Humiliation, on the other hand, degrades the soul, warping and deforming it; it irritates, impoverishes, and blights, inflicting a moral hurt most ill to heal.

There is not, I believe, one single deformation or deviation of character—these kinks that make so many of Dostoevsky's characters so strangely morbid and disturbing —but which has its beginning in some humiliation.

The Insulted and Injured is the title of one of his first books, and his work as a whole is obsessed without ceasing by the idea that humiliation damns, whereas humility sanctifies. Heaven, as Alyosha Karamazov dreams and describes it to us, is a world where there will be no injured, neither insulted.

The strangest, most disturbing figure of these novels, the terrible Stavrogin in *The Possessed*, whose character at first is so different from all others, is explained, and his demoniac nature accounted for, by certain passages in the book:

"Nikolay Vsyevolodovitch Stavrogin," says one of the other characters, "was leading at that time in Petersburg a life, so to say, of mockery. I can't find another word to describe it, because he is not a man who falls into disillusion-ment, and he disdained to be occupied with work at that time."[1]

And Stavrogin's mother, to whom these remarks were addressed, says a little farther on:

"No, it was something more than eccentricity, and I assure you, something sacred even! A proud man who has suffered humiliation early in life and reached the stage of 'mockery,' as you so subtly called it."[2]

And later:

"And if Nikolay had always had at his side (Varvara Petrovna almost shouted) a gentle Horatio, great in his humility—another excellent expression of yours, Stephan Trofimovitch!—he might long ago have been saved from the sad and sudden demon of irony, which has tormented him all his life."[3]

It happens that some of Dostoevsky's characters, whose natures have been profoundly warped by humiliation, find as it were delight and satisfaction in the resultant degradation, loathsome though it be.

"Was there resentment in my heart?" says the hero of *A Raw Youth* just when his amour-propre had been cruelly wounded, "I don't know. Perhaps there was. Strange to say, I always had, perhaps from my earliest childhood, one characteristic; if I were ill-treated, absolutely wronged and insulted to the last degree, I always showed at once an

---

[1] *The Possessed*, p. 172.   [2] *Ibid.*, p. 175.   [3] *Ibid.*, p. 175.

irresistible desire to submit passively to the insult, and even to accept more than my assailant wanted to inflict on me, as though I would say: 'All right, you have humiliated me, so I will humiliate myself even more; look and enjoy it.' "[1]

For if humility be a surrender of pride, humiliation, on the other hand, but serves to strengthen it.

Listen to the tale told by the wretched hero of 'the *Notes from Underground*:

"One night, as I was passing a tavern, I saw through a lighted window some gentlemen fighting with billiard cues, and saw one of them thrown out of the window. At other times, I should have felt very much disgusted, but I was in such a mood at the time, that I actually envied the gentleman thrown out of the window—and I envied him so much that I even went into the tavern and into the billiard-room. 'Perhaps,' I thought, 'I'll have a fight, too, and they'll throw me out of the window.'

"I was not drunk—but what is one to do?—depression will drive a man to such a pitch of hysteria! But nothing happened. It seemed that I was not even equal to being thrown out of the window, and I went away without having my fight.

"An officer put me in my place from the first moment. I was standing by the billiard-room tables and in my ignorance blocking up the way, and he wanted to pass; he took me by the shoulders and without a word, without warning or explanation, moved me from where I was standing to another spot and passed by as though he had not noticed me. I could have forgiven blows, but I could not forgive his having moved me without noticing me.

"Devil knows what I would have given for a real, regular quarrel—a more decent, a more literary one, so to

[1] *A Raw Youth*, p. 327.

speak. I had been treated like a fly. This officer was over six foot, while I was a spindly little fellow. But the quarrel was in my hands. I had only to protest and I certainly would have been thrown out of the window. But I changed my mind, and preferred to beat a resentful retreat."[1]

But if we carry the story further, we shall soon see the excess of hatred to be nothing other than love inverted.

". . . I often met that officer afterwards in the street, and noticed him very carefully. I am not quite sure whether he recognized me: I imagine not, I judge from certain signs. But I—I stared at him with spite and hatred, and so it went on—for several years! My resentment grew even deeper with years. At first I began making stealthy inquiries about this officer. It was difficult for me to do so, for I knew no one. But one day I heard one shout his name in the street as I was following him at a distance, as though I was tied to him,— and so I learned his surname. Another time I followed him to his flat, and for ten kopecks learned from the porter where he lived, on which storey, whether he lived alone or with others, and so on—in fact, everything one could learn from a porter. One morning, though I had never tried my hand with the pen, it suddenly occurred to me to write a satire on this officer in the form of a novel which would unmask his villainy; I even exaggerated it; at first I so altered his sur- name that it could not easily be recognized, but on second thoughts I changed it, and sent the story to the O.Z.

"But at that time such attacks were not the fashion and my story was not printed. That was a great vexation to me. Sometimes I positively choked with resentment. At last I determined to challenge my enemy to a duel. I composed a splendid, charming little letter to him, imploring him to apologize to me, and hinting rather plainly at a duel in case of refusal. The letter was so composed that if the officer had

[1] *Notes from Underground*, pp. 86–7.

had the least understanding of the good and beautiful, he would certainly have flung himself on my neck and offered his friendship. And how fine that would have been! How we should have got on together!"[1]

So often in Dostoevsky one particular feeling is suddenly supplanted in this way by its direct opposite! We can find example after example of it. For instance, that unhappy child (in *The Karamazovs*) biting with hatred into Alyosha's finger when the latter holds out his hand to him, just at the time when the child, though he does not recognize it, is developing for the same Alyosha a shy, wild affection.

And what, in this young child, could have caused such a warping of affection?

He had seen Dmitri Karamazov, Alyosha's brother, come drunk out of an inn, thrash his father, and pull him insolently by the beard: "Papa, papa, how he humiliated you!" he cried later.

Thus, over against humility—on the same moral plane, if I may be permitted to say so, but at the other extreme of the scale—there is pride, which humiliation exaggerates, exasperates, and deforms, sometimes hideously.

Certainly, psychological axioms appear to Dostoevsky for what they really are: special definitions of truth. As novelist (for Dostoevsky is no mere theoretician, he is an explorer) he steers clear of introduction and realizes how imprudent (on his part, at least) any attempts to formulate general laws would be.[2] It is for us to discover these laws in his books, by cutting, as it were, paths through the thicket. Here is one of the laws we can establish: the man

[1] *Notes from Underground*, pp. 88–9.

[2] "However adventurous the Russian genius," wrote Boris de Schloezer in the *Nouvelle Revue Française*, February 1922, "it characteristically chooses a firm foundation in concrete fact and living reality: this basis once assured, it launches out into speculation of the most abstract and daring nature, returning in the end, rich with the gathered spoils of thought, to the fact and reality from which it started and in which it is perfected."

who has suffered humiliation seeks to inflict humiliation in his turn.[1]

Despite the extraordinarily rich diversity of his *Comédie Humaine*, Dostoevsky's characters group and arrange themselves always on one plane only, that of humility and pride. This system of grouping discomfits us; indeed, at first, it appears far from clear, for the very simple reason that we do not usually approach the problem of making a diversion at such an angle and that we distribute mankind in hierarchies. Let me explain my idea: in Dickens's wonderful novels, for instance, I am often uneasy at the conventionality, childishness even, of his *hierarchy*, or to use Nietzsche's phrase, *scale of values*. While reading him I have the impression that I am contemplating one of Fra Angelico's *Last Judgements* where you have the redeemed, the damned, and the indeterminate (not too numerous!) over whom angel and demon struggle. The balance that weighs them all, as in an Egyptian bas-relief, reckons only the positive or negative quality of their virtue. Heaven for the just: for the wicked, Hell. Herein Dickens is true to the opinion of his countrymen and of his time. It does happen that the evil prosper, while the just are sacrificed—to the great shame of this earthly existence and of society as we have organized it. All his novels endeavour to show us and make us realize the shining superiority of qualities of heart over qualities of head. I have selected Dickens as a type because of all the great novelists we know he uses this classification in its simplest form: which—if I may say in conclusion—is the secret of his popularity.

Now, after reading in close succession practically all Dostoevsky's works, I have the impression that there exists in them, too, a similar classification: less apparent, no

---

[1] E.g. Lebedyev in *The Idiot*. See Appendix (2), the admirable chapter describing Lebedyev's enjoyment in torturing General Ivolgin.

doubt, although almost as simple, and, in my estimation, much more significant. For it is not according to the positive or negative quality of their virtue that one can *hierarchize* (forgive me this horrible word!) his characters: not according to their goodness of heart, but by their degree of pride.

Dostoevsky presents on one side the humble (some of these are humble to an abject degree, and seem to enjoy their abasement); on the other, the proud (some to the point of crime). The latter are usually the more intelligent. We shall see them, tormented by the demon of pride, ever striving after something higher still:

"There, I'll bet anything—that you've been sitting side by side in the drawing-room all night wasting your precious time discussing something lofty and elevated," says Stavrogin to the abominable Pyotr Stepanovitch in *The Possessed*.[1] Or again:

"In spite of the terror which I detected in her myself, Katerina Nikolaevna has always from the first cherished a certain reverence and admiration for the nobility of Andrey Petrovitch's principles and the loftiness of his mind. . . . In his letter he gave her the most solemn and chivalrous promises that she should have nothing to fear—she responding with the same heroic feelings. There may have been a sort of chivalrous rivalry on both sides."[2]

"There is nothing in it to fret your vanity," said Elizabeth to Stavrogin: "The day before yesterday when I 'insulted' you before everyone and you answered me so chivalrously, I went home and guessed at once that you were running away from me because you were married, and not from contempt for me, which, as a fashionable young lady, I dreaded more than anything," adding by way of conclusion, "Anyhow, it eases our vanity."[3]

[1] *The Possessed*, p. 495.   [2] *A Raw Youth*, p. 507.
[3] *The Possessed*, pp. 489–90.

His women, even more so than his characters of the other sex, are ever moved and determined by considerations of pride. Look at Raskolnikov's sister, Nastasya Filippovna and Anglaïa Epantchin in *The Idiot*, Elizabeth Nikolaïevna in *The Possessed*, and Katerina Ivanovna in *The Karamazovs*!

But, by an inversion which I make bold to describe as inspired by the New Testament, the most abject characters are nearer the Kingdom of Heaven than the noblest. To such a degree is Dostoevsky's work dominated by these profound truths. *"God resisteth the proud, but giveth grace to the humble."*—*"For the Son of man is come to save that which was lost."*

On the one hand, denial and surrender of the self; on the other, affirmation of the personality, the *will to power*, an exaggerated loftiness of sentiment. And take due note of this fact; in Dostoevsky's novels, the *will to power* leads inevitably to ruin.

M. Souday recently accused me of sacrificing, indeed, of immolating Balzac to Dostoevsky. Need I protest? My admiration of Dostoevsky is certainly fervent, but I do not think I am blinded by it. I readily agree that Balzac's creations surpass the Russian novelist's in their diversity, and that his *Comédie Humaine* is the more varied. Dostoevsky certainly goes deeper and touches more important points than any other author, but we can admit that his characters are one and all cut from the same cloth. Pride and humility! these hidden reagents never change, although by graduating the doses of them, we obtain reactions that are infinitely rich and minutely varied in colour.

With Balzac (as invariably in Western society, in French especially, to which his novels hold a mirror) two factors are active which in Dostoevsky's work practically do not exist: first, the intellect, second, the will. I do not pretend that in Balzac will-power always urges a man towards what is good, and that his strong-willed characters are never but virtuous. But at least consider how many of his characters attain to what is of good repute by effort of will and open up a glorious career by dint of perseverance, cleverness, and determination. Think of his David Séchards, his Bianchons, Joseph Brideaus, and Daniel d'Arthez—and there are twenty such I could name!

In all Dostoevsky we have not a single great man. "But what about that splendid Father Zossima in *The Karamazovs?*" you may say. Yes, he is certainly the noblest figure the Russian novelist had drawn; he far and away dominates the whole tragedy, and once we have entered into possession of the promised complete version of *The Karamazovs*, we shall understand still better his importance. At the same time we shall realize what in Dostoevsky's eyes constitutes his real greatness. Father Zossima is not of the great as the world reckons them. He is a saint—no hero! And he has reached saintliness by surrender of will and abdication of intellect.

If I examine along with Balzac's the resolute characters that Dostoevsky presents, I suddenly realize what terrible creatures they are, one and all. Look at Raskolnikov, heading the list; in his beginnings, a miserable worm—with ambitions, who would like to be a Napoleon, and only attains to being the murderer of an old broker-woman and of an innocent girl. Look at Stavrogin, Pyotr Stepanovitch, Ivan Karamazov, the hero of *A Raw Youth* (the only one of Dostoevsky's characters who, from his earliest days, at least since consciousness dawned, lived with a fixed determination, to wit, in this case, of becoming a Rothschild, and, by mockery as it were, in all the books of Dostoevsky nowhere is there a more pithless creature, at the mercy of his fellow-beings, individually and collectively). His heroes' determination, every particle of cleverness and will-power they possess, seem but to hurry them onward to perdition, and if I seek to know what part mind plays in Dostoevsky's novels, I realize that its power is demonic.

His most dangerous characters are the strongest intellectually, and not only do I maintain that the mind and the will of Dostoevsky's characters are active solely for evil, but that, when urged and guided towards good, the virtue to which they attain is rotten with pride and leads to destruction. Dostoevsky's heroes inherit the Kingdom of God only by the denial of mind and will and the surrender of personality.

We can without hesitation affirm that Balzac, too, is, to a certain degree, a Christian author. But only by confronting the two ethical points of view, the French author's and the Russian's, can we realize the chasm between the former's Catholicism and the latter's purely evangelical doctrine, and how widely the Catholic spirit can differ from the purely Christian. Or, to offend none, let me express myself thus: Balzac's *Comédie Humaine* sprang from the contact between the Gospels and the Latin mind: Dostoevsky's from the contact between the Gospels and Buddhism, the Asiatic mind.

These are merely preliminary considerations which will help us at our next meeting to probe deeper into the souls of these strange creations.

III

WHAT we have accomplished so far has been a mere clearing of the ground. Before attacking the problem of Dostoevsky's philosophy, I should like to warn you against a grave misconception. During the last fifteen years of his life, Dostoevsky busied himself considerably with the editing of a review. The articles he wrote for this periodical have been collected in what is known as the *Journal of an Author*. In these articles Dostoevsky sets forth his ideas. It would seem the simplest and most natural thing in the world to make constant reference to this book; but I may as well admit at once that it is profoundly disappointing. In it we find an exposé of his social theories, which, however, never emerge from the nebulous state and are most awkwardly expressed. We find, too, political prophecies not one of which has come true. Dostoevsky tries to foretell the future state of Europe and goes far astray in practically every instance.

M. Souday, who recently devoted one of his literary reviews in the *Temps* to Dostoevsky, takes a delight in pointing out his mistakes. In these articles of Dostoevsky's he sees nothing more than journalism of the most everyday type, which fact I am prepared to concede. But I do protest when he goes on to say that these same articles are a wonderful revelation of Dostoevsky's ideas. As a matter of fact, the problems Dostoevsky handles in his *Journal of an Author* are not the problems that interest him most. Political questions are frankly less important in his estimation than social problems, these in turn far less important than moral and individual problems. The rarest and deepest truths we can expect from him are psychological, and I add that in this province the ideas he submits are most often left in the problematic state, in the form of a question. He is seeking not so much a solution as an exposition of these very questions which, by reason of their complexity, confusion, and interdependence, are as a rule left ill-defined. In a word, Dostoevsky is not, strictly speaking, a thinker; he is a novelist. His favourite theories, and all that is subtle and novel in them, must be sought in the speeches of his characters, and not always in those of his most important ones. It often happens that his most valuable and daring ideas are attributed to subordinate characters. Dostoevsky is awkwardness itself when speaking in his own name. To his own case might well be applied the sentence he puts into Versilov's mouth. "Explain?" he said. "No, it's better not to; besides, I've a passion for talking without explanations. That's really it. And there's another strange thing; if it happens that I try to explain an idea I believe in, it almost always happens that I cease to believe what I have explained."[1]

We can even say that it is exceptional for Dostoevsky not to turn against his own theory as soon as formulated. It seems as if for him it immediately breathed an odour of decay, like that which emanated from Father Zossima's dead body—the body expected to work miracles—and made the death-watch so painful for Alyosha Karamazov, his disciple.

It is evident that for a philosopher this feature would be something of a drawback. His ideas are practically never absolute, remaining relative always to the characters expressing them. I shall press the point even further and assert their relativity not merely to these characters, but to a specific moment in the lives of these characters. The ideas are, as it were, the product of a special and transitory state of his *dramatis personæ*, and relative they remain, subservient to and

[1] *A Raw Youth*, p. 215.

conditioned by the particular fact or action which determines them or by which they are determined. As soon as Dostoevsky begins to theorize, he disappoints us. Thus even in his article, *Of the Nature of Lying*,[1] despite his prodigious skill in exhibiting falsehood in all its forms and making us realize thereby what prompts the untruthful to their falsehoods (and how differently he proceeds from Corneille!), as soon as he begins to account for it all, as soon as he theorizes on the strength of his examples, he becomes stale and unprofitable.

This *Journal* is proof that Dostoevsky's genius is essentially as a novelist, for although in theoretical or critical articles he never rises above mediocrity, he becomes excellent as soon as a character appears on the scene. It is in this *Journal* that we come across these admirable tales of *The Peasant Marey*[2] and *Krotchkaya*,[3] the latter outstandingly fine and powerful, in its way a novel that is really but one long monologue, like the *Notes from Underground*, written about the same period.

Better still, or rather, more significant, are the two instances in this *Journal* when Dostoevsky allows us to watch the almost involuntary, almost subconscious activity of his mind engaged in the construction of a narrative.

After he tells us his delight in watching people walking in the streets and occasionally in following them, we see him suddenly attach himself to a chance passer-by:

"I notice a workman passing; he has no wife leaning on his arm, but he has a child with him, a little boy. Both are sad and lonely looking. The man is about thirty years of age: his face is worn and of an unhealthy tinge. He is wearing his Sunday best, a top-coat, rubbed at the seams and with buttons worn almost bare of cloth. The collar of the coat is very soiled, the trousers are cleaner, but look as if

[1] See the *Journal*.   [2] Garnett, Vol. XI.   [3] *Ibid.*, Vol. X.

they had come straight from the broker's. His top-hat is very shabby. I have the idea he is a printer. His expression is hard, gloomy, almost sullen. He holds the boy by the hand; the youngster lags behind a little. The child is two, or not much more, very pale and delicate looking, neatly dressed in a tunic, little boots with red uppers, and a hat tricked out with a peacock's feather. He is weary. The father speaks to him, making fun maybe of his feeble little legs. The youngster makes no reply, and a few paces farther on, his father bends down, lifts him up in his arms and carries him. The child seems pleased, and throws his arms round his father's neck. He catches sight of me, and from his perch stares down at me in astonishment and curiosity. I give him a little nod, but he frowns and clings closer still to his father's neck. They must love each other dearly, these two!

"In the streets I love to watch the passers-by, gaze into their unknown features, guess their identity, imagine how they exist and what can be their interest in life. To-day I have eyes for none but this father and child. I imagine that the wife and mother had died not long since, that the father is busy working the whole week in the shop, while the child is left to the care of some elderly woman. They probably live in a basement where the father rents or even only shares a room, and to-day, being Sunday, the father is taking the boy to see some relative, the mother's sister probably. I'm sure this aunt of whom they don't see much must be married to a non-commissioned officer and live in the basement of the barracks, but in a separate apartment. She mourns her dead sister, but not for long. The widower does not show much grief either, during this visit anyway. He remains preoccupied, has little to say for himself, and replies only to personal questions. Soon he falls silent altogether. Then the samovar is brought in and they all take tea. The boy is left sitting on a bench in the corner, shy and frowning, and he finally drops off to sleep. The aunt and her husband take scant notice of him, except for passing him a cup of milk and a piece of bread. The husband, with not a word to say for himself at first, comes out suddenly with a coarse joke, savouring of the barrack-room, and makes fun of the youngster whom his father begins to scold. The child wants to leave at once, and the father fetches him home from Vyborg to Liteinyi.

"To-morrow the father will be back at his workshop, and the youngster left once more with the old woman."[1]

In another passage of the same book,[2] we read an account of his meeting with a woman a hundred years old. As he passed along the street, he noticed her sitting on a bench. He spoke to her, then went on his way. But in the evening, after the day's work was done, the old woman came back to his mind. He imagined her home-coming and what her family said to her. He describes her death: "I take a delight in inventing the end of the story. Besides, I am a novelist and I love telling stories."

Besides, Dostoevsky never invents by chance. In one of the articles in the same *Journal*, à propos of the Kornilov trial, he reconstitutes and rebuilds the story in his own way, and after the process of the law has thrown light on every aspect of the crime, he writes: "I divined almost everything," and adds: "Chance enabled me to go and see Madame Kornilova. I was astonished to see that my suppositions were almost identical with the true facts. I had, I admit, made a few errors of detail: for instance, Kornilov, though from the country, wore the townsman's dress, etc.," and Dostoevsky concludes: "All in all, my errors have been slight; the basis of my suppositions remains accurate."[3]

With such gifts as an observer, such powers as a narrator

[1] Bienstock and Nau, pp. 99–100.   [2] *Ibid.*, pp. 176–81.
[3] *Ibid.*, pp. 294 et seq., 450–2.

and reconstructor of actual events, and an added degree of sensitiveness, you can make a Gogol or a Dickens. Perhaps you remember the beginning of the *Old Curiosity Shop* where Dickens, too, is busy following up the passers-by, and after he has left them, goes on to imagine their lives? But such gifts, remarkable as they are, do not wholly account for a Balzac, a Thomas Hardy, a Dostoevsky. They would certainly not suffice to make Nietzsche write: "Dostoevsky was the only psychologist from whom I had anything to learn; he belongs to the happiest windfalls of my life, happier even than the discovery of Stendhal."[1]

Long ago I copied from Nietzsche a page I should like to read to you. When he wrote it, had Nietzsche not in view what constitutes the essential value of the great Russian novelist, what opposes him diametrically to many of our modern novelists, to the Goncourts, for example, whom Nietzsche seems to indicate in these lines? "*A Moral for Psychologists!*—Do not go in for any notebook psychology! Never observe for the sake of observing! Such things lead to a false point of view, to a squint, to something forced and exaggerated! To experience things on purpose—this is not a bit of good. In the midst of an experience a man should not turn his eyes upon himself; in such cases any eye becomes the evil eye. A born psychologist instinctively avoids seeing for the sake of seeing. And the same holds good of the born painter. Such a man never works 'from Nature'—he leaves it to his instinct, to his camera obscura to sift and to define the 'fact', 'nature', the 'experience'. The general idea, the conclusion, the result is the only thing that reaches his consciousness. He knows nothing of that wilful process of deducing from particular cases. What is the result when a man sets about the matter differently?—When, for instance,

[1] Nietzsche, *The Twilight of the Idols*, translated by Anthony M. Ludovici, 1911, p. 104.

after the manner of Parisian novelists, he goes in for note-book psychology on a large and small scale? Such a man is constantly spying on reality, and every evening he bears home a handful of fresh curios. . . . But look at the result!"[1]

Dostoevsky never observes for observation's sake. His work is not the result of observations of the real; or at least, not of that alone. Nor is it the fruit of a preconceived idea, and that is why it is never mere theorizing, but remains steeped in reality. It is the fruit of intercourse between fact and idea, a blending, in the proper English sense of the word, of the one with the other, so perfect that it can never be said that one element outweighs the other. Hence the most realistic scenes in his novels are the most pregnant with psychological and moral import. To be precise, each work of Dostoevsky's is produced by the crossing of fact and idea. "The germ of the novel has been in me for the last three years," he wrote in 1870,[2] referring to *The Brothers Karamazov*, not written until nine years later. In another letter he says: "The chief problem dealt with throughout this particular work is the very one which has, my whole life long, tormented my conscious or subconscious being: the question of the existence of God."[3]

But the idea is present only cloudily in his mind until it comes into contact with some fact from real life (in this instance, a criminal court case, a *cause célèbre*) which will make it fructify. Then—and not till then—can we speak of the work as conceived. "I am writing with a purpose," he says in the same letter, speaking of *The Possessed* which reached fruition about the same period as *The Karamazovs*, another novel with a purpose. Nothing less gratuitous, in the modern acceptation of the term, than Dostoevsky's

[1] Nietzsche, *The Twilight of the Idols*, translated by Anthony M. Ludovici, 1911, pp. 64–5.
[2] Bienstock, p. 367. Letter to N. N. Strakhov, Dresden, March 24, 1870.
[3] *Ibid.*, p. 374. Letter to A. N. Maïkov, Dresden, March 25, 1870.

work. Each of his novels is in its way a demonstration, I might even say a speech for the defence, or better still, a sermon. And if I dared find in this wonderful artist any grounds for reproach, I might suggest that he sought to *prove* only too well.

Let there be no disagreement on this score: Dostoevsky never tries to influence our opinion unduly. He seeks to bring light into dark places, to make plain certain hidden truths, which to him appear already dazzlingly clear and of paramount importance, the most important, no doubt, to which the mind of man can attain: not truths of an abstract nature, beyond human grasp, but truths secret and intimately personal. On the other hand, what saves his work from the disfigurements inseparable from all writing with a purpose, is the fact that these truths are ever subordinated to fact, and his ideas infused with reality. Towards these realities of human experience, his attitude is ever humble and obedient; he never applies pressure nor turns a happening to his own advantage. It would seem that even to his very thought he applied the Gospel precept: *"For whosoever will save his life shall lose it; but whosoever will lose his life for My sake, the same shall save it."*

Before attempting to trace some of Dostoevsky's ideas in his books, I should like to speak of his method of working. Strakhov tells us that Dostoevsky worked almost exclusively at night: "About midnight, when everything was becoming still, there was Dostoevsky left alone with his samovar, and he used to go on working till five or six in the morning, sipping at intervals cold, mild-drawn tea. He rose about two or three in the afternoon, spent the rest of the day entertaining   guests,   walking,   or   visiting   friends." Dostoevsky was not always able to content himself with mild-drawn tea; during the last years of his life, he lost grip of himself, and drank, we are told, a great quantity of spirits.

One day, so the story runs, Dostoevsky came out of his study, where he was busy writing *The Possessed*, in a state of remarkable mental exhilaration, obtained in some degree by artificial stimulus. It was Madame Dostoevsky's "at home" day. Dostoevsky, wild-eyed, burst into the drawing-room where several ladies were sitting, one of whom, cordiality itself, hastened forward to him with a cup of tea. "Devil take you and your dish-water," he shouted.

You remember Abbé de Saint-Réal's words?—and meaningless they might well appear did not Stendhal make use of them as a cover for his own æsthetic principles: "A novel is the mirror of one's walks abroad." In France and in England the novels that can be classed under this rubric are numerous indeed. What of Lesage, Voltaire, Fielding, Smollett? But nothing could be more remote from this category than a novel of Dostoevsky's. Between his novels and those of the authors quoted above, aye, and Tolstoy's too, and Stendhal's, there is all the difference possible between a picture and a panorama. Dostoevsky composes a picture in which the most important consideration is the question of light. The light proceeds from but one source. In one of Stendhal's novels, the light is constant, steady, and well-diffused. Every object is lit up in the same way, and is visible equally well from all angles; there are no shadow effects. But in Dostoevsky's books, as in a Rembrandt portrait, the shadows are the essential. Dostoevsky groups his characters and happenings, plays a brilliant light upon them, illuminating one aspect only. Each of his characters has a deep setting of shadow, reposes on its own shadow almost. We notice in Dostoevsky a strange impulse to group, concentrate, centralize: to create between the varied elements of a novel as many cross-connections as possible. With him, events instead of pursuing their calm and measured course, as with Stendhal or Tolstoy, mingle and confuse in turmoil; the elements of the story—moral, psychological, and material—sink and rise again in a kind of whirlpool. With him there is no attempt to straighten or simplify lines; he is at his happiest in the complex; he fosters it. Feelings, thoughts, and passions are never presented in the pure state. He never isolates them. And now I come to make an observation on Dostoevsky's manner of drawing his characters. But first of all let me read these very pertinent remarks of Jacques Rivière's: "Once the idea of a character has taken shape in his mind, a novelist has to choose between two ways of materializing it. He can either insist on its complexity, or emphasize its cohesiveness; in this soul he is about to create, he can deliberately reproduce its absolute darkness, or for the reader he can dispel such darkness by his very description of it; he will either respect the soul's hidden depths, or lay them open."

You see what Rivière's theory is: the French school explores the unplumbed depths, whereas certain foreign novelists, Dostoevsky in particular, respect and cherish their gloom.

"In any case," Rivière continues, "it is these black gulfs that interest Dostoevsky most, and his whole effort is directed towards suggesting how utterly unreachable they are. . . . We, on the other hand, faced with a soul's complexity and endeavouring to give a picture of it, instinctively seek to organize our material." Serious enough! But there is more to come. "At need, we force things a trifle; we suppress a few small divergencies, and interpret certain obscure details in the sense most useful towards establishing a psychological unity. The ideal we strive towards is the complete closing up of every gulf."[1]

I am not so sure that we do not find some gulfs in Balzac,

---

[1] *Nouvelle Revue Française*, February, 1922, pp. 176-7.

inexplicably abrupt; nor am I sure either that Dostoevsky's are as unfathomed as at first would be imagined. Shall I give you an example of Balzac's gulfs? I see one in *La Recherche de l'absolu*. Balthazar Claès is seeking the philosopher's stone: apparently he has completely forgotten the religious training of his childhood. He is absorbed by his quest. He neglects his wife, Josephine, whose religious mind is horror-stricken at her husband's disbelief. One day she enters the laboratory without warning. The draught of the opening door causes an explosion, and Madame Claès falls fainting. . . . What is the cry that escapes Balthazar's lips? One wherein suddenly reappears his childhood's belief, long overlaid by the dross of his atheism. "Thank God you're still alive! The Saints have preserved you from death!" Balzac does not press the incident any further, and no doubt nineteen out of every twenty readers will never even detect the fault. The abyss of which it gives a glimpse is left unexplained: maybe no explanation is possible. As a matter of fact, that was of no interest to Balzac. His one concern was to produce characters free of all inconsequences, wherein he was in perfect accord with French feeling; for what we French require most of all is logic.

I can say with respect not only to the *Comédie Humaine*, but also to the comedy of everyday life as we live it, that the *dramatis personæ* (for we French delineate ourselves as we see ourselves) are after a Balzacian ideal. The inconsequences of our nature, should such exist, seem to us awkward and ridiculous. We deny them. We try to ignore them, to palliate them. Each of us is conscious of our unity, our continuity even, and everything we repress and thrust beneath our consciousness, like the feeling that suddenly reasserts itself in Claès, we try to suppress completely, and failing this, we cease to hold it of any account. We consistently behave as the character we are—or fancy we are—

ought to behave. The majority of our actions are dictated, not by the pleasure we take in doing them, but by the need of imitating ourselves and projecting our past into the future. We sacrifice truth (that is to say, sincerity) to purity and continuity of line.

And in face of all this, what does Dostoevsky offer? Characters that, without any thought for consistency, yield with facility to every contradiction and negation of which their peculiar constitution is capable. This seems to be Dostoevsky's chief interest—inconsequence. Far from concealing it, he emphasizes and illuminates it without ceasing.

There is admittedly much that he fails to explain. I do not think there is much that could not be explained were we prepared to concede, as Dostoevsky invites us to do, that man is the dwelling-place of conflicting feelings. Such cohabitation seems often in Dostoevsky the more paradoxal in that his characters' feelings are forced to their extremest intensity and exaggerated to the point of absurdity.

I believe it right to press this point, for you may be thinking that this is an old story, just the conflict between passion and duty as we see it in Corneille. The problem is really different. The French hero, as Corneille depicts him, throws before himself the image of an ideal: there is not a little of himself in it, himself as he desires and strives to be, not as Nature made him, or as he would be if he yielded to his instincts. The inward struggle Corneille pictures is the fight between the ideal being to which the hero tries to conform, and the natural being, which he seeks to deny. In short, we are not so far removed in this instance from what Jules de Gaultier terms *bovarysm*—a name given, after Flaubert's heroine, to the tendency of certain human beings towards complementing their real life by a purely imaginary existence, in which they cease to be what they are and become what they would like to be.

Every hero, every man who is not content merely to drift, but struggles towards some ideal and tries to achieve it, offers us an example of this *bovarysm*.

What we find in Dostoevsky, the examples of dual existence submitted to us, how far different are they! They have no connection, or at least but little, with the frequently observed pathological states, where a second personality is grafted upon the original, the one alternating with the other and two groups of sensations and associations of ideas being formed, the one unknown to the other, so that ere long we have two distinct personalities sharing the one fleshly tenement. They change places, the one succeeding the other in turn, all the time ignorant of its neighbour. Think how admirably Stevenson illustrates this condition in his phantastic tale of the *Strange Case of Dr. Jekyll and Mr. Hyde.*

But in Dostoevsky the most disconcerting feature is the simultaneity of such phenomena, and the fact that each character never relinquishes consciousness of his dual personality with its inconsistencies.

It so happens that one of his heroes, in great stress of feeling, is uncertain whether it is love or hate that moves him, for these opposing emotions are mingled and confounded within him.

"And suddenly a strange surprising sensation of a sort of bitter hatred for Sonia passed through his (Raskolnikov's) heart. As it were wondering and frightened of this sensation, he raised his head and looked intently at her; but he met her uneasy and painfully anxious eyes fixed on him: there was love in them; his hatred vanished like a phantom. It was not the real feeling—he has taken the one feeling for the other."[1]

Of this misinterpretation of feeling by the person concerned we should find examples in Marivaux, and in Racine as well.

[1] *Crime and Punishment*, p. 369.

At times one of these feelings exhausts itself by its very exaggeration. It seems as if the expression of the feeling disconcerts the character expressing it. With this we are not yet come to duality of feeling; but here is something more definite! Listen to Versilov, the *Raw Youth's* father:

"If only I were a weak-willed nonentity and suffered from the consciousness of it! But you see that's not so. I know I am exceedingly strong, and in what way do you suppose? Why, just in that spontaneous power of accommodating myself to anything whatever, so characteristic of all intelligent Russians of our generation. There's no crushing me, no destroying me, no surprising me. I've as many lives as a cat. I can with perfect convenience experience two opposite feelings at one and the same time, and not, of course, through my own will."[1]

"I do not undertake to account for this co-existence of conflicting feelings," deliberately says the narrator in *The Possessed*.

Versilov goes on to say: "I should like to say something nice to Sonia, and I keep trying to find the right word, though my heart is full of words which I don't know how to utter; do you know I feel as if I were split in two?"—He looked round at us all with a terribly serious face and with perfectly genuine candour.—"Yes, I am really split in two mentally, and I'm horribly afraid of it. It's just as though one's second self were standing beside one; one is sensible and rational oneself, but the other self is impelled to do something perfectly senseless, and sometimes very funny; and suddenly you notice that you are longing to do that amusing thing, goodness knows why; that is, you want to, as it were, against your will; though you fight against it with all your might, you want to. I once knew a doctor who suddenly began whistling in church, at his father's funeral.

[1] *A Raw Youth*, pp. 205-6.

I really was afraid to come to the funeral to-day, because, for some reason, I was possessed by a firm conviction that I should begin to laugh or whistle in church, like that unfortunate doctor, who came to rather a bad end. . . ."[1]

Listen now to Stavrogin, the strange hero of *The Possessed*: "I am still capable, as I always was, of desiring to do something good, and of feeling pleasure from it; at the same time I desire evil and feel pleasure from that too."[2] As Baudelaire says, no man but is ever entreating God and the Devil at one and the same time.[3]

With the help of some passages from William Blake, I shall try to throw some light on these apparent contradictions, and especially on Stavrogin's strange declaration. But this attempt at explanation I shall hold over till later.

---

[1] *A Raw Youth*, p. 503. Compare this other passage (*ibid.*, p. 548) dealing with one of these pathological cases I mentioned a little space ago. "Versilov can have had no definite aim, and I believe, indeed, he did not reflect on the matter at all, but acted under the influence of a whirlwind of conflicting emotions. But the theory of actual madness I cannot accept, especially as he is not in the least mad now. But the 'second self' I do accept unquestionably. What is the second self exactly? The second self, according to a medical book, written by an expert, which I purposely read afterwards, is nothing else than the first stage of serious mental derangement, which may lead to something very bad."

[2] *The Possessed*, p. 635.

[3] *Journaux Intimes*, p. 57.

IV

AT our last meeting we noticed the disquieting duality by which most of Dostoevsky's characters are racked and driven, and which prompts Raskolnikov's friend to say à propos of the hero of *Crime and Punishment*: "It really looks as if there were in him two opposite natures showing themselves in turn."

And were these natures never visible but in turn, all would still be well, but we have seen how they often come to manifest themselves simultaneously. We have watched each of these contradictory impulses exhausted, depreciated, and inhibited by its own expression and manifestation, giving way to its opposite, and the hero is never nearer love than when he has just given exaggerated expression to his hatred, never nearer hatred than in the exaggeration of his love.

In all Dostoevsky's creations, in his women characters especially, we detect an uneasy presentiment of their own instability. The dread of being unable to maintain for long the same mood or resolve drives them often to disconcertingly abrupt action. For instance, Lizaveta in *The Possessed* makes up her mind with great alacrity, because she knows from long experience that her resolutions never last more than a minute.

To-day I propose to study some of the results of this strange duality; but first of all let me ask whether this duality really exists, or whether Dostoevsky only imagines it? Does life provide him with any examples? Is it observed from Nature, or does he merely obligingly yield to his imaginative bent?

Nature, according to Oscar Wilde's *Intentions*, copies the model set her by Art, and this apparent paradox he delights in illustrating by several specious insinuations, the gist of his argument being that Nature—"as you will not have failed to observe"—has taken to imitating Corot's landscapes nowadays!

His meaning is undoubtedly that, accustomed to looking at Nature in a manner that is become conventional, we recognize only what Art has educated us to discern. When a painter essays to transmute and express in his work a personal vision, Nature's new aspect seems at first brush paradoxal, insincere, freakish even. However, we speedily grow used to contemplating her with the bias given by this new method, and recognize only what the artist pointed out to us. Hence, to eyes unprejudiced, Nature would really seem to *imitate* Art.

What I have said about painting applies equally to novels and the intimate landscapes of psychology. We exist on given premises, and readily acquire the habit of seeing the world, not so much as it actually is, but as we have been told and persuaded it is. How many diseases were non-existent, so to speak, until diagnosed and described! How many strange, pathological, abnormal states we identify round us, aye, within us, once our eyes have been opened by reading Dostoevsky! Yes, I firmly believe he opens our eyes to certain phenomena;—I do not necessarily mean rare ones, but simply phenomena to which we had been so far blind.

Faced with the complexity almost every human being offers, the eye tends inevitably, spontaneously, unconsciously almost, to simplify to some extent.

Such is the French novelist's instinctive effort. He singles out the chief elements in a character, tries to discern clearcut lines in a figure and reproduce the contours unbroken. Whether Balzac or another, no matter: the desire, the need, even, for *stylization* is all-important. None the less I believe it would be a gross mistake—one to which I fear many a foreigner is prone—to scorn and discredit the psychology of French literature on account of the sharp outlines it presents, the complete absence of indistinctness, and the lack of shading.

Remember that Nietzsche with rare perspicacity recognized and proclaimed the extraordinary superiority of our French psychologists, judging them—and to an even greater degree perhaps our moralists—Europe's most eminent masters. True that in the eighteenth and nineteenth centuries we had authors of unrivalled analytical powers: I have our moralists chiefly in mind. But I am not wholly satisfied that our present-day novelists are able to compete with them, for here in France we have an unfortunate habit of keeping to formulæ which soon become mechanical, and of resting content with them instead of pressing onwards.

I have already remarked elsewhere that La Rochefoucauld, while rendering splendid service to psychology, had in a measure arrested its development by reason of the very perfection of his *Maxims*. I must apologize for quoting myself, but I should find some difficulty in improving on these lines I wrote in 1910:

"When La Rochefoucauld bethought himself of reducing and ascribing every generous impulse of the human heart to the solicitations of personal vanity, I doubt whether it was not less a proof of rare insight than a check to further and more pertinent investigation. The formula, once found, was strictly adhered to, and for two hundred years people lived content with this interpretation. The most sceptical of psychologists passed as the most highly enlightened could he but detect in the noblest, most forgiving actions the hidden promptings of selfishness—losing sight thereby of all that is contradictory in the human soul. I do not make bold to criticize La Rochefoucauld's impeachment of personal vanity, but I most definitely take exception to his limiting himself to this one consideration and believing that with *amour propre* the final word had been spoken. I blame still more his successors for carrying the question no further."[1]

Throughout French literature we find a horror of the formless, a certain impatience with what is not yet formed. This is how I account for the very small place taken by the child in French novels as compared with English or Russian. Scarcely a child is to be met with in our novels, and such authors as do introduce children—all too infrequently at that—are more often than not conventional, awkward, and dull.

In Dostoevsky's works children are numerous, and it is worth noting that the majority of his characters—and of these the most important—are still young, hardly set. It seems to be the genesis of feelings that interests him chiefly, for he depicts them as indistinct, in their larval state, so to speak.

He has a predilection for baffling cases that challenge accepted psychology and ethics. It is plain that in the midst of everyday morality and psychology he himself does not feel at his ease. His temperament clashes painfully with certain rules accepted as established, which neither please nor satisfy him.

We find a similar uneasiness and lack of satisfaction in Rousseau. We know that Dostoevsky was an epileptic and that Rousseau went mad. I shall dwell later on the function of the morbid state in shaping their thought. Let us rest content to-day with recognizing in this abnormal physiological condition an invitation, as it were, to rebel against the psychology and the ethics of the common herd.

In man are many things unexplained, aye, unexplainable maybe, but once we admit the duality I discussed a moment ago, we cannot but admire the logic with which Dostoevsky

[1] André Gide, *Morceaux Choisis*, pp. 102-3.

pursues its consequences. In the first place, note that nearly all Dostoevsky's characters are polygamists; I mean that by way of satisfying, doubtless, the complexity of their natures, they are almost all capable of several attachments simultaneously. Another consequence, and, if I may use the term, corollary to this argument, is the practical impossibility of producing jealousy. These creatures simply do not know what jealousy means!

Consider, first of all, the cases of multiple attachments he puts before us. Prince Myshkin is divided between Aglaïa Epantchin and Nastasya Filippovna. "I love her with my whole heart," he says, referring to Nastasya.

"And at the same time you have declared your love for Aglaïa Ivanovna?"

"Oh, yes, yes."

"How so? Then you must want to love both of them?"

"Oh, yes, yes."

"Upon my word, Prince, think what you are saying. . . . Do you not know what, the most likely thing is that you have never loved either of them! And how can you love two at once? That's interesting!"[1]

And each of the two heroines is likewise torn between two loves. Think too of Dimitri Karamazov between Grushenka and Natasya Ivanovna, and do not forget Versilov. Many another instance I could quote!

You may think one of their loves was of the flesh, the other of the spirit. Much too obvious a solution, I consider. Besides, on this score, Dostoevsky is never perfectly straightforward. He leads us on to numerous suppositions, then leaves us in the lurch. It was not until I was reading *The Idiot* for the fourth time that I became conscious of a fact now plain as daylight: all the whims and moods in Madame Epantchin's attitude towards Prince Myshkin, all the

[1] *The Idiot*, pp. 587–8.

hesitancy of Aglaïa, her daughter and the Prince's betrothed, might well be due to the intuition these two women had (the mother in particular, of course) of some mystery in his character, and to their uncertainty whether he could prove an effectual husband. Dostoevsky lays stress several times on Prince Myshkin's chastity, and doubtless this very chastity filled Madame Epantchin, his future mother-in-law, with uneasiness.

"There is no doubt that the mere fact he could come and see Aglaïa without hindrance, that he was allowed to talk to her, sit with her, walk with her, was the utmost bliss to him; and who knows perhaps he would have been satisfied with that for the rest of his life. It was just this contentment that Lizaveta Prokofyevna (Madame Epantchin) secretly dreaded. She understood him; she dreaded many a thing in secret, which she could not have put into words herself."[1]

And note what to me seems most important: in this instance, as indeed frequently, the less physical love is the stronger.

I have no wish to force Dostoevsky's idea. I do not suggest that divided love and absence of jealousy open up the way to complaisant community of possession, at least not always, no, nor necessarily: they lead rather to renunciation. But, as I reminded you, Dostoevsky is not over frank on this subject. . . .

The question of jealousy preoccupied Dostoevsky unceasingly. In one of his first books, *Another Man's Wife,* we find this paradox: Othello must not be looked upon as a typical example of real jealousy. Perhaps it behoves us to see in this contention nothing more than an urgent desire to go against current opinion.

But later on Dostoevsky comes back to the point, and

[1] *The Idiot,* p. 519.

speaks again of Othello in *A Raw Youth,* one of his last books. "Versilov said once that Othello did not kill Desdemona and afterwards himself because he was jealous, but because he had been robbed of his ideal."[1]

Is this really a paradox? I recently came across a similar assertion in Coleridge—the similarity is so marked that I wonder if Dostoevsky had not perchance been familiar with it.

"Othello does not kill Desdemona in jealousy, but in a conviction forced upon him by the almost superhuman art of Iago. . . . Othello had no life but in Desdemona: the belief that she, his angel, had fallen from the heaven of her native innocence, wrought a civil war in his heart. . . . But yet the pity of it, Iago. Oh, Iago, the pity of it!"

Constitutionally incapable of jealousy, then, Dostoevsky's heroes? Perhaps I am going a little too far, or, at least, it would be seemly to modify my statement slightly. It may be said that of jealousy these creatures know only the suffering it brings, a suffering which is not complicated by any feeling of hatred for their rivals: this point is of primary importance. If hatred there be, as in the *Eternal Husband,* which case we shall examine presently, the hatred is counterbalanced and restrained by a strange, imperious affection for the rival. But most frequently there is no suspicion of hatred, nor even suffering. And now we are venturing on a precipitous path where we have every chance of overtaking Jean-Jacques Rousseau, equably tolerating the favours shown by Madame de Warens to his rival, Claude Anet, or, his thoughts full of Madame d'Houdetot, writing in his *Confessions*:

"Anyway, no matter how ardent the passion I had conceived for her, I found it as sweet to be the confidant as to be the object of her affections, and never for a moment did I consider her lover as my rival, I always held him my friend.

[1] *A Raw Youth,* p. 253.

(He refers to Saint-Lambert.) People will say that is not love: maybe not, perhaps it is more than love."

Similarly, in *The Possessed*, we are told that Stavrogin, far from feeling jealous, developed a great friendship for his rival.

At this point I propose a short detour to help us probe the question more deeply and grasp Dostoevsky's conception. When I recently re-read most of his novels, I was fascinated by Dostoevsky's manner of passing from one book to another. Undoubtedly it was natural that after *The House of the Dead* he should write Raskolnikov's story in *Crime and Punishment*, the story of the crime that sent the latter to Siberia. More absorbing still to watch how the last pages of this novel lead up to *The Idiot*. You remember we left Raskolnikov in Siberia so completely regenerated in mind that he said the happenings of his past life had lost all importance for him: his crimes, his repentance, his martrydom, even, seemed to him like the life-history of a stranger.

"He was simply feeling. Life had stepped into the place of feeling."[1] This is the frame of mind in which we find Prince Myshkin at the beginning of *The Idiot*, a frame of mind which could be, and in Dostoevsky's eyes doubtless was, the Christian state *par excellence*. I shall revert to this point.

Dostoevsky seems to establish in the human soul—or simply recognizes as already existing—a kind of stratification. I can distinguish in the characters of his novels three strata or regions. First the intellectual, remote from the soul and whence proceed the worst temptations. Therein dwells, according to Dostoevsky, the treacherous demonic element. For the moment I am concerned only with the second region, the region of passion, ravaged and desolated by storms; but tragic though the happenings be that these storms determine, the very soul of Dostoevsky's characters

[1] *Crime and Punishment*, p. 492.

is scarcely affected. There is a region deeper still, where passion exists not. This is the region that resurrection (and I grant the word the full significance bestowed on it by Tolstoy), re-birth, in Christ's words, enables us to reach as Raskolnikov reached it. In this region Myshkin lives and moves.

The transition from *The Idiot* to the *Eternal Husband* is more interesting still. You surely remember that at the close of *The Idiot* we leave Prince Myshkin at the bedside of Nastasya Filippovna whom her lover Rogozhin, the prince's rival, has just murdered. There stand the rivals, face to face, close to each other. Will they kill each other? No, indeed! They weep together, and spend a wakeful night stretched out side by side at the foot of Nastasya's bed.

"Every time the delirious man (Rogozhin) broke into screaming or babble, he hastened to pass his trembling hand softly over his hair and cheeks, as though caressing and soothing him."[1]

Almost the theme of *The Eternal Husband*! *The Idiot* dates from 1868, *The Eternal Husband* from 1870. Some men of letters—and as clever a critic as Marcel Schwob was amongst them—consider the latter novel Dostoevsky's masterpiece. His masterpiece! Perhaps that is excessive. But, at any rate, it is *a masterpiece*, and it is interesting to hear what Dostoevsky himself had to say about the book.

"I have a story," he wrote to his friend Strakhov on March 18, 1869, "not a very long one. I had already thought of writing it three or four years ago, the year my brother died, encouraged by some words of Apollon Gregoriev who, praising my *Notes from Underground*, said to me, 'Just write something in this style.' But it will be something quite different, as far as form goes: the foundation, however, will still be the same. My everlasting theme . . . I can write the

---

[1] *The Idiot*, p. 616.

story very quickly, because there is not a word or line of it but what is clear to me. It is already written in my head, although nothing is down on paper so far."[1]

And in a letter dated October 27, 1869, he continues:

"Two-thirds of the story are almost completely written and recopied. I've done my best to cut it down, but that was impossible. It is not a question, though, of quantity, but of quality. Of its quality I cannot speak, for I have no notion myself: others will decide that point."[2]

And here is what others have to say:

"Your short story," writes Strakhov, "is making a very lively impression here, and will, in my opinion, have an unchallenged success. It is one of the best worked-out of your novels, and by reason of its subject, one of the most interesting you have ever written. I am speaking of Trusotsky: the majority will have difficulty in understanding this character, but the book is being read and will be read eagerly."

Notes from Underground appeared a short time before this volume. I believe that with these *Notes* we reach the height of Dostoevsky's career. I consider this book (and I am not alone in my belief) as the keystone of his entire works. But with it we return to the intellectual region, so I shall not speak further of it to-day. Let us linger with *The Eternal Husband* in the realm of passion. In this short tale there are but two characters, the husband and the lover. Concentration could be carried no further. The whole book responds to an ideal we should nowadays call classical: the action itself, or at least the initial fact that provokes the drama, had already taken place, as in one of Ibsen's plays.

Velchaninov is come to that time of life when the past begins to look different to his eyes:

[1] Bienstock, pp. 319–20.
[2] *Ibid.*, p. 343. Letter to A. N. Maïkov, Dresden, October 27, 1869.

"Now that he was verging on the forties, the brightness and good humour were almost extinguished. These eyes, which were already surrounded by tiny wrinkles, had begun to betray the cynicism of a worn-out man of doubtful morals, a duplicity, an ever-increasing irony, and another shade of feeling, which was new: a shade of sadness and of pain—a sort of absent-minded sadness as though about nothing in particular, and yet acute. This sadness was specially marked when he was alone."[1]

What is happening with Velchaninov? What *does* happen at this age, at this turning point in life? So far, we have had the joy out of life; but suddenly we realize that our actions, the happenings we have brought about, once separated from us and launched out into the world, like a skiff on the sea, continue a separate existence often unknown to us. George Eliot speaks admirably of this in *Adam Bede*. Yes, the events in his own past no longer appear to Velchaninov in quite the same light, because he suddenly realizes his *responsibility*. At this period he meets one whom he knew in bygone days, the husband of a woman who had been his mistress. This husband appears in rather whimsical fashion. It is impossible to decide whether he is avoiding Velchaninov or pursuing him. He seems to spring up without warning from between the very paving stones in the street. He wanders around mysteriously, haunting the vicinity of Velchaninov's house, unrecognized at first.

I shall not attempt to recount the gist of the book, nor how after a late night visit from Pavel Pavlovitch Trusotsky, the husband, Velchaninov decides to call upon him. Their standpoints, obscure at first, become clearer:

" 'Tell me, Pavel Pavlovitch, you are not alone here, then? Whose little girl is that I found with you just now?'

"Pavel Pavlovitch was positively amazed and raised his

eyebrows, but he looked frankly and pleasantly at Velchaninov.

" 'Whose little girl? Why, it's Liza!' he said, with an affable smile.

" 'What Liza?' muttered Velchaninov, with a sort of inward tremor. The shock was too sudden. When he came in and saw Liza, just before, he was surprised, but had absolutely no presentiment of the truth, and thought nothing particular about her.

" 'Yes, our Liza, our daughter Liza!' Pavel Pavlovitch smiled.

" 'Your daughter? Do you mean that you and Natalya Vassilyevna had children?' Velchaninov asked timidly and mistrustfully in a very low voice.

" 'Why, of course! But there, upon my word, how should you have heard of it? What am I thinking about! It was after you went away God blessed us with her!'

"Pavel Pavlovitch positively jumped up from his chair, in some agitation, though it seemed agreeable too.

" 'I heard nothing about it,' said Velchaninov, and he turned pale.

" 'To be sure, to be sure, from whom could you have heard it?' said Pavel Pavlovitch, in a voice weak with emotion, 'My poor wife and I had lost all hope, as no doubt you remember, and suddenly God sent us this blessing, and what it meant to me He only knows! Just a year after you went away, I believe. No, not a year, not nearly a year. Wait a bit—why, you left us, if my memory does not deceive me, in October or November, I believe.'

" 'I left T—— at the beginning of September, the twelfth of September, I remember it very well.'

" 'In September, was it? H'm! what was I thinking about'? cried Pavel Pavlovitch, much surprised. 'Well, if that's so, let me see, you went away on the twelfth of September, and

Liza was born on the eighth of May, so—September—
October—November—December—January—February—
March—April—a little over eight months! And if you only
knew how my poor wife . . .'

" 'Show me—call her,' Velchaninov faltered in a breaking
voice."[1]

And thus Velchaninov learns that his passing whim, by
which he had set so little store, has left its mark. At once the
question presents itself—does the husband know? Almost
to the very end of the book the reader is left in doubt.
Dostoevsky keeps us undecided, and this very indecision tortures Velchaninov. He does not know where he
is. Or rather, it seems to us early in the day that Pavel
Pavlovitch knows, but feigns ignorance, precisely in order to
torture the lover by the indecision he skilfully maintains in
his mind.

Here is one way of considering this strange book. *The
Eternal Husband* depicts the struggle between genuine and
sincere feeling on one hand, and conventional feeling,
accepted and current psychology on the other.

"There is but one way out—a duel," cries Velchaninov.
But you realize what a base issue that is, bringing satisfaction
to no existing feeling, and simply pandering to an artificial
conception of honour, one I touched on lately, a Western
conception, for which we have no use here. We soon realize
that, in his heart of hearts, Pavel Pavlovitch hugs his very
jealousy. Yes, he positively loves and welcomes his suffering.
This eagerness to suffer played already an important part in
Notes from Underground.

In France, where the Russians are concerned, there has
been much talk, in imitation of De Vogüé, of a *religion of
suffering*. We French love to hear a formula, and to use one!
It is one easy way of naturalizing an author and assigning

---

[1] *The Eternal Husband*, pp. 35–6.

him to his place in the show-case. Our mind likes precise data to hold fast by; and once satisfied, what need for thought or personal contact?—Nietzsche? Oh, yes! "The *superman*. Be ruthless. Live dangerously."—Tolstoy? "Non-resistance to evil."—Ibsen? "Northern mists."—Darwin? "Man is decended from the monkey. The struggle for life."—D'Annunzio? "The religion of beauty." Woe betide the authors whose ideas refuse to be reduced to a formula! The bulk of the reading public simply cannot tolerate them (and Barrès realized this when to his merchandise he affixed the label: *La Terre et les Morts*).

Yes, in France we tend to deceive ourselves with words, and believe that everything possible has been achieved and that it is time to apply the closure and pass on, once the formula has been found. In the same way we believed victory already in our grasp, thanks to Joffre and his "wearing down the enemy," or to Russia and her "steam-roller advance."

A *religion of suffering* . . . let us eliminate at once the possibility of misinterpretation. It is not a question, or rather not solely a question, of vicarious suffering, the world-wide suffering before which Raskolnikov humbles himself to lie at Sonia the prostitute's feet, or Father Zossima at Dmitri Karamazov the predestined parricide's, but a theory of personal suffering.

Throughout the whole book, Velchaninov keeps asking himself whether Trusotsky is jealous or not, whether he knows all or nothing. The question is absurd: of course Trusotsky knows! Of course he is jealous, but with the jealousy he fosters and cherishes within himself. It is the torment of jealousy that Trusotsky desires and enjoys, just as we saw the attachment of the hero of the *Underground* to his toothache.

Of the hideous torment of the jealous husband we learn practically nothing. Dostoevsky reveals it only indirectly, by

virtue of the cruel suffering Trusotsky inflicts on the
creatures round about him, especially on the little girl whom
he adores in spite of all. The child's anguish helps us to
measure the intensity of the father's own suffering. Pavel
Pavlovitch tortures the child, whom he loves passionately;
he can no more hate her than he can hate his wife's lover:

" 'Do you know what Liza has been to me?'—he suddenly
recalled the drunkard's exclamation and felt that that exclamation was sincere, not a pose, and that there was love in it.
How could that monster be so cruel to a child whom he
loved so much? Is it credible? But every time he made haste
to dismiss that question, and, as it were, brush it aside; there
was something awful in that question, something he could
not bear and could not solve."[1]

We may rest assured that the keenest of his suffering is due
to his instability to become jealous: of jealousy he has only
the suffering, and he cannot hate the man who was preferred
to himself. The very sufferings he inflicts on his rival, those
he would fain inflict upon him, the torments he inflicts on his
little daughter, are a kind of mystic counterpart that he sets
to the horror and the anguish in whose depths he is struggling. None the less, he dreams of revenge: not that he has
any precise desire to avenge himself, but he tells himself that
he must seek revenge, as perhaps the sole means of freeing
himself from such awful torments.

"Habit is everything, even in love," says Vauvenargues,[2]
and you remember La Rochefoucauld's maxim? "*How many
men would never have known love if they had never heard of love?*"
Are we not justified in asking: How many would never be
jealous, if they did not hear jealousy spoken about, and had
not persuaded themselves that it was imperative to be
jealous?

[1] *The Eternal Husband*, p. 75.
[2] *Vauvenargues*, Maxim xxxix; *Œuvres*, p. 377.

Yes, convention is the great breeder of falsehood. How many are forced to play their life long a part strangely foreign to themselves? And how difficult it is to discern in ourselves a feeling not previously described, labelled, and present before us as a model! Man finds it easier to imitate everything than to invent anything. How many are content to live their lives warped by untruth, and find, none the less, in the very falsity of convention more comfort and less need for effort than in straightforward affirmation of their personal feelings! Such affirmation would require of them an effort of invention utterly beyond them.

" 'I'll tell you a killing little anecdote, Alexey Ivanovitch,' said Trusotsky. 'I thought of it this morning in the carriage. I wanted to tell you of it then. You said just now "hangs on people's necks." You remember perhaps Semyon Petrovitch Livstov, he used to come and see us when you were in T——: well, his younger brother, who was also a young Petersburg swell, was in attendance on the Governor at V——, and he too was distinguished for various qualities. He had a quarrel with Gobulenko, a colonel, and considered himself insulted, but he swallowed the affront and concealed it, and meanwhile Gobulenko cut him out with the lady of his heart and made her an offer. And what do you think? This Livstov formed a genuine friendship with Gobulenko, he quite made it up with him, and, what's more, insisted on being his best man: he held the wedding crown and when they came out from under it, he went up to kiss and congratulate Gobulenko. And in the presence of the Governor and all the honourable company, with his swallow-tail coat, and his hair in curl, he sticks the bridegroom in the stomach with a knife—so that he rolled over! His own best man! What a disgrace! And, what's more, when he'd stabbed him like that, he rushed about crying: "Alas, what have I done! Oh, what is it that I've done!"

with floods of tears, trembling all over, flinging himself on people's necks, even ladies. "Ah, what have I done!" he kept saying, "what have I done now!" He—he—he! he was killing. Though one feels sorry for Gobulenko, perhaps, but after all, he recovered.'

" 'I don't see why you told me this story,' observed Velchaninov, frowning sternly.

" 'Why, all because he stuck the knife in him, you know,' Pavel Pavlovitch tittered. . . ."[1]

And in similar fashion, Pavel Pavlovitch's real spontaneous feeling expresses itself, when he is unexpectedly obliged to nurse Velchaninov, down with a liver complaint.

"The sick man fell asleep suddenly, a minute after lying down. The unnatural strain upon him that day, in the shattered state of his health, had brought on a sudden crisis, and he was as weak as a child. But the pain asserted itself again and weariness; and an hour later he woke up and painfully got up from the sofa. The storm had subsided, the room was full of tobacco smoke, on the table stood an empty bottle, and Pavel Pavlovitch was asleep on another sofa. He was lying on his back, with his head on the sofa cushion, fully dressed and with his boots on. His lorgnette had slipped out of his pocket, and was hanging down almost to the floor."[2]

Strange how Dostoevsky, when leading us through the strangest by-paths of psychology, ever must needs add the most precise and infinestimal of realistic details, in order to make more secure an edifice which otherwise would appear the extreme expression of phantasy and imagination.

Velchaninov is in great pain, and immediately Trusotsky applies every possible means of alleviating it.

"But Pavel Pavlovitch, goodness knows why, seemed beside himself a though it were a question of saving his own

[1] *The Eternal Husband*, pp. 65–6.   [2] *Ibid.*, pp. 116–17.

son. Without heeding Velchaninov's protests, he insisted on the necessity of compresses and also of two or three cups of weak tea to be drunk on the spot, 'and not simply hot, but boiling.' He ran to Mavra, without waiting for permission, with her laid a fire in the kitchen, which always stood empty, and blew up the samovar; at the same time he succeeded in getting the sick man to bed, took off his clothes, wrapped him up in a quilt, and within twenty minutes had prepared tea and compresses.

" 'This is a hot plate, scalding hot!' he said, almost ecstatically, applying the heated plate, wrapped up in a napkin, on Velchaninov's aching chest. 'There are no other compresses, and plates, I swear on my honour, will be even better; they were laid on Pyotr Kuzmitch, I saw it with my own eyes, and did it with my own hands. One may die of it, you know. Drink your tea, swallow it; never mind about scalding yourself! Life is too precious for one to be squeamish.'

"He quite flustered Mavra, who was half asleep; the plates were changed every two or three minutes. After the third plate, and the second cup of tea, swallowed at a gulp, Velchaninov felt a sudden relief.

" 'If once they've shifted the pain, thank God, it's a good sign!' said Pavel Pavlovitch, and he ran joyfully to fetch a fresh plate and a fresh cup of tea.

" 'If only we can ease the pain, if only we can keep it under!' he kept repeating.

"Half an hour later the pain was much less, but the sick man was so exhausted that, in spite of Pavel Pavlovitch's entreaties, he refused to put up with 'just one more nice little plate.' He was so weak that everything was dark before his eyes.

" 'Sleep, sleep!' he repeated in a faint voice.

" 'To be sure,' Pavel Pavlovitch assented.

" 'You'll stay the night—what time is it?'

" 'It's nearly two o'clock, it's quarter to.'

" 'You'll stay the night?'

" 'I will, I will.'

"A minute later the sick man called Pavel Pavlovitch again. 'You, you,' he muttered, when the latter had run up and was bending over him: 'You are much better than I am! I understand it all—all. . . . Thank you.'

" 'Sleep, sleep,' whispered Pavel Pavlovitch, and he hastened on tiptoe to his sofa.

"As he fell asleep, the invalid heard Pavel Pavlovitch noiselessly making a bed for himself, and taking off his clothes. Finally, putting out the candle, and almost holding his breath for fear of waking the patient, he stretched himself on his sofa."[1]

And yet, a quarter of an hour later, Velchaninov catches Trusotsky, who believes him sound asleep, bending over him with intent to murder him.

"Pavel Pavlovitch wanted to kill him, but didn't know he wanted to kill him! 'It's senseless, but that's the truth,' thought Velchaninov."[2]

And yet he is not satisfied!

" 'And can it be that it was all true?' he exclaimed again, suddenly raising his head from the pillow and opening his eyes. 'All that madman told me yesterday about his love for me, when his chin quivered and he thumped himself on the breast with his fist?'

" 'It was the absolute truth,' he decided, still pondering and analysing. 'That quasimodo from T—— was quite sufficiently stupid and noble to fall in love with the lover of his wife, about whom he noticed nothing suspicious in twenty years! He had been thinking of me with respect,

[1] *The Eternal Husband*, pp. 117-18.
[2] *Ibid.*, p. 124.

cherishing my memory and brooding over my "utterances" for nine years. Good Heavens! And I had no notion of it! He could not have been lying yesterday. But did he love me yesterday when he declared his feeling and said, "Let us settle our account!" Yes, it was from hatred that he loved me; that's the strongest of all loves. . . .

". . . Only he didn't know then whether he would end by embracing me or murdering me. Of course, it's turned out that the best thing was to do both. A most natural solution'."[1]

If I have lingered so long over this slender book, it is because it is more accessible than the rest of Dostoevsky's novels, and helps us to win, beyond love and hate, to that wider region I spoke about not long since: a region where love is not, nor passion, so easily and so simply reached: the region Schopenhauer spoke of, the meeting-place of human brotherhood, where the limits of existence fade away, where the notion of the individual and of time is lost, the place wherein Dostoevsky sought—and found—the secret of happiness.

[1] *The Eternal Husband*, pp. 124–6.

V

AT our last meeting I spoke of the three strata or regions Dostoevsky seems to discern in the human personality: first, the province of intellectual speculation, then the domain of the passions, midway between the former and the third region, a vast realm remote from the play of passion.

It is plain that these three strata are not isolated or even strictly limited, but interpenetrate.

The intermediate region, the domain of passion, I have already discussed. Here, and on this plane, the play is staged, not merely the play Dostoevsky presents in each of his works, but the drama of entire mankind. We observed, too, what at first wore the air of a paradox: no matter how restless and powerful, the passions after all are of but slender importance, or at least do not stir the soul's utmost depths. Events have no hold on the soul—they are simply without its province. To support my assertion, what instance could I more aptly adduce than war? Investigations have been carried out in regard to the terrible struggle through which we have but lately passed. Literary men were asked to estimate its real or apparent moment, its moral after-effects, its influence on literature. The answer is simple: to all intents and purposes its influence has been nil.

Consider for a moment the Napoleonic wars: endeavour to trace their repercussion in literature and determine in what way they have modified the soul of humanity. I admit there exist poems inspired by the imperial epic as there exist only all too many with the Great War for theme. But where is there a deeper note, a spiritual transformation? No exterior event, whatever its tragedy or magnitude, can effect such a change. On the other hand, the French Revolution is different, but here we are concerned with a disturbance that is more than physical, a traumatism, if I may use the word. This time the convulsion proceeds from the very soul of the nation. The influence of the French Revolution on the writings of Montesquieu, Voltaire, and Rousseau is enormous, although their works date from before the event for which they prepared the way. And we shall observe the same order of things in Dostoevsky's novels: the idea is not consecutive to the event, but precedes it. In most cases passion has to serve as intermediary between thought and action.

At any rate, in Dostoevsky's novels we shall see that the intellectual element comes at times into touch with that deeper region, which is not the soul's hell, but its heaven.

In Dostoevsky we find the mysterious inversion of values already noticed in William Blake, the great mystic amongst English poets. Hell, according to Dostoevsky, is the first region, the realm of mind and reason. Throughout his works, if our attention be at all alert, we shall become conscious of a depreciation of mental powers which is not so much systematic as involuntary and inspired by the spirit of the Gospel.

Dostoevsky never deliberately states, although he often insinuates, that the antithesis of love is less hate than the steady activity of the mind. In his eyes it is intellect which individualizes, which is the enemy of the Kingdom of Heaven, life eternal, and that bliss where time is not, reached only by renouncing the individual self and sinking deep in a solidarity that knows no distinctions.

This passage from Schopenhauer will prove illuminating: "He sees that the difference between him who inflicts suffering and him who must bear it is only phenomenon; and does not concern the thing in itself, for this is the will living in both, which here deceived by the knowledge which is bound to its service, does not recognize itself, and seeking an increased happiness in *one* of its phenomena, produces great suffering in *another*, and thus, in the presence of excitement, buries its teeth in its own flesh, not knowing that it always injures only itself, revealing in this form, through the medium of individuality, the conflict with itself, which it bears in its inner nature. The inflicter of suffering and the sufferer are one. The former errs in believing that he is not a partaker in the guilt. If the eyes of both were opened, the inflicter of suffering would see that he lives in all that suffers pain in the wide world, and which if endowed with reason, in vain asks why it was called into existence for such great suffering, its desert of which it does not understand, and the sufferer would see that all the wickedness which is, or ever was, committed in this world, proceeds from that will which constitutes *his* nature also, appears also in *him*, and that through this phenomenon and its assertion he has taken upon himself all the sufferings which proceed from such a will, and bears them as his due, so long as he *is* this will."[1]

But this pessimism (which in Schopenhauer can at times virtually have the air of a disguise) yields place in Dostoevsky to a boundless optimism.

"If you were to give me three lives, it wouldn't be enough for me,"[2] says one of his characters in *A Raw Youth*. In another passage of the same book:

"You so want to live and are so thirsting for life that I do believe three lives would not be enough for you."[3]

I should like to investigate further this blissful state Dostoevsky depicts, or of which he gives us a glimpse, in

[1] Schopenhauer, *The World as Will and Idea*, translated by Haldane and Kemp; Bk. IV, p. 457.

[2] *A Raw Youth*, p. 68.   [3] *Ibid.*, p. 130.

each of his works, a state wherein we lose all sense of personal limitation and of the flight of time.

"At that moment," said Prince Myshkin to Rogozhin, "I seem somehow to understand the extraordinary saying that there shall be no more time."[1]

And compare this eloquent passage from *The Possessed*:

" 'Are you fond of children?' asked Stavrogin.—'I am,' answered Kirillov, though rather indifferently.—'Then you are fond of life?'—'Yes, I'm fond of life. What of it?'— 'Though you've made up your mind to shoot yourself?'— 'What of it? Why connect it? Life's one thing, and that's another. Life exists, but death doesn't at all.'—'You've begun to believe in future eternal life?'—'No, not in a future eternal life, but eternal life here. There are moments, you reach moments, and time suddenly stands still and it will become eternal.' "[2]

I could multiply my quotations, but these doubtless will suffice.

I am struck, every time I read the Gospels, by the insistence with which the words, "*Et nunc*," "*And now*," are repeated over and over again. And certainly Dostoevsky too was struck by it. Everlasting bliss, the bliss promised by Jesus Christ, can be attained here and now, if only the human soul will forswear and deny itself. *Et nunc.* . . .

Eternal life is not, or rather is more than, a thing of the future, and if we do not reach it in this world, there is little hope of our ever attaining to it. Listen to these admirable pages from Mark Rutherford's *Autobiography*:

"As I got older, I became aware of the folly of this perpetual reaching after the future, and of drawing from to-morrow—and from to-morrow only—a reason for the joyfulness of to-day. I learned, when, alas! it was almost too late, to live in each moment as it passed over my head,

[1] *The Idiot*, p. 225.   [2] *The Possessed*, p. 219.

believing that the sun as it is now rising is as good as it ever will be, and blinding myself as much as possible to what may follow. But when I was young I was the victim of that illusion, implanted for some purpose or other in us by Nature, which causes me on the brightest morning in June to think immediately of a brighter morning which is to come in July. I say nothing now for or against the doctrine of immortality. All I say is, that men have been happy without it, even under the pressure of disaster, and that to make immortality a sole spring of action here is an exaggeration of the folly which deludes us all through life with endless expectation, and leaves us at death without the thorough enjoyment of a single hour."

Cheerfully would I cry: "What betides life eternal, without ever-present consciousness of that eternity even now? Eternal life can be present in us here below. We are partakers in it from the moment we are resigned to die to ourselves and accomplish the surrender which enables us to resurrect straightway into eternity!"

Neither behest nor ruling: simply the secret of the supreme felicity revealed by Jesus Christ in the Gospels. "*If ye know these things, happy are ye if ye do them*" (John xiii. 17). Not "*happy shall ye be*" but "*happy are ye.*" Here and now we can share in that perfect bliss.

What serenity! Time indeed ceases to exist: eternity lives, we inherit the Kingdom of God.

Yes, here is the mysterious essence of Dostoevsky's philosophy and of Christian ethics too; the divine secret of happiness. The individual triumphs by renunciation of his individuality. He who lives his life, cherishing personality, shall lose it: but he who surrenders it shall gain the fullness of life eternal, not in the future, but in the present made one with eternity. Resurrection in the fullness of life, forgetful of all individual happiness.—Oh! perfect restoration!

Such glorification of feeling and inhibition of thought is nowhere better indicated than in the following passage from *The Possessed* which complements the one I read a few moments since:

"'You seem to be very happy, Kirillov,' said Stavrogin.

"'Yes, very happy,' he answered, as though making the most ordinary reply.

"'But you were distressed so lately, angry with Liputin?'

"'H'm! . . . I'm not scolding now, I didn't know then I was happy. Have you seen a leaf, a leaf from a tree?'

"'Yes.'

"'I saw one lately, a little green. It was decayed at the edges. It was blown by the wind. When I was ten years old I used to shut my eyes in the winter on purpose and fancy a green leaf, bright, with veins on it, and the sun shining. I used to open my eyes and not believe them because it was very nice, and I used to shut them again.'

"'What's that? An allegory?'

"'N-no. . . . Why? I'm not speaking of an allegory, but of a leaf, only a leaf. The leaf is good: everything's good.'

"'When did you find out you were so happy?'

"'Last week, on Tuesday—no, Wednesday, for it was Wednesday by that time, in the night.'

"'By what reasoning?'

"'I don't remember. I was walking about the room . . . never mind. I stopped my clock. It was thirty-seven minutes past two.'"[1]

But, you may well contend, if feeling is to overcome thought, and the soul know no state but this vague expectancy susceptible to every outside influence, what can result except complete anarchy? It has been said, and of late more frequently, that anarchy is the consummation of Dostoevsky's doctrine. A discussion of his beliefs would

[1] *The Possessed*, pp. 220, 221.

lead us into a far country, for I can anticipate the storm of
protest I should provoke if I dared affirm that Dostoevsky
does not plunge us into anarchy, but simply and naturally
leads us to the Gospels. On this point we must be clear.
Christian doctrine as contained in the New Testament is
usually seen by people of our nation through the medium of
the Roman Catholic Church, as she has modified it, moreover, in harmony with her own needs. Now, Dostoevsky
abhors all churches, the Church of Rome in particular. He
claims it his right to accept Christ's teaching directly from
the Scriptures, and from them alone, which is precisely what
the Catholic cannot possibly concede.

In his letters we come across countless passages inveigh-
ing against the Roman Catholic Church, accusations so
vehement and so categorical that I dare not repeat them to
you here. But they confirm the general impression I gather at
each fresh reading of Dostoevsky and help me to a better
understanding of him. I know no author at once more
Christian and less Catholic in spirit.

"But you have put your finger on the very crux of the
question," Roman Catholics will say, "and you have yourself explained it, many and many a time, seemingly with full
understanding. The Gospels, the words of our Lord Jesus
Christ, considered apart, lead but to anarchy, whence the
need for St. Paul, for the Church, for Catholicism as a
whole. . . ." I shall not attempt to argue with them.

Dostoevsky leads us, we may take it, if not to anarchy, to
a sort of Buddhism, or at least *quietism*, and we shall see that
in the judgment of the orthodox, this is not his only heresy.
He draws us far away from Rome—the Rome of the
Encyclicals, I mean—far, too, from worldly codes of honour.

"But look here, Prince, are you a man of honour?"
cries one of his characters to Prince Myshkin, the hero who
best embodied his philosophy until the day when he wrote

The Karamazovs and presented to us these angelic creatures, Alyosha and Father Zossima. What then does Dostoevsky exalt as his ideal? The life contemplative? A life wherein man, renouncing reason and will, shall know love alone?

Perhaps Dostoevsky would find personal happiness in such an existence, but certainly not man's higher destiny. As soon as Prince Myshkin, far from his native land, reaches the higher plane, he is urgently impelled to turn his steps homeward, and when young Alyosha confides to Father Zossima his secret aspirations towards ending his days in the monastry, his confessor says to him: "Go hence from this house, thou wilt be of greater use out in the world! Thy brothers have need of thee!" . . . "*I pray not that thou shouldest take them out of the world, but that thou shouldest keep them from evil.*"

I notice (and with this remark I come to treat of the demonic element in Dostoevsky's works) that most translations of the Bible render Jesus's words "*But deliver them from evil,*" which is not quite accurate. The translations I mean are Protestant versions. Protestantism is inclined to leave out of the reckoning angel and demon alike. By way of experiment I have often asked Protestants if they believed in the Devil, and invariably my question has been received with bewilderment. Then I realized that in most cases this was a question the Protestant had never put to himself. In the end he replied that he did, of course, believe in evil, and when I pressed him, he admitted that in evil he discerned only the absence of good, as in darkness the absence of light. Now, we are here far removed indeed from the Gospel texts which mention time and again a diabolic force, real, present, and defined. "*Deliver them from evil?*" . . . No! "*Deliver them from the Evil One.*" This problem of the Devil occupies, I may say, an important place in Dostoevsky's work. Some no doubt will see in him a Manichean. We are aware that the great heresiarch, Mani, recognized two principles controlling the universe—the Power of Good and the Power of Evil, equally active, independent and indispensable, by which belief the Manichean doctrine is directly associated with the teaching of Zarathustra. We observed (and on this point I am bound to insist) how Dostoevsky assigns the Devil's habitation, not to the baser elements in man, but to the very noblest—the realm of intellect, the seat of reason, although man's entire being even can become the Archfiend's dwelling-place and prey. The most cunning snares laid for us by the Evil One are, in Dostoevsky's reckoning, intellectual temptations and problems. I do not think it will be going far astray from my subject if I consider first of all the problems expressing mankind's torturing obsessions. . . . What is Man? Whence comes he and whither does he return? What was he before birth, what becomes of him after death? To what Truth can mankind attain?—or even more pertinently—What *is* Truth?

With Nietzsche a new problem arose, completely different from the rest, and far from being absorbed amongst these others, it pressed straight to the forefront. As a problem it, too, has its torturing uncertainty—an uncertainty that drove Nietzsche to madness. "What can mankind accomplish? What can one single man accomplish?" The question implies the terrible apprehension that man could have been other than he is, could have accomplished—could yet accomplish greater things, whereas he is content to take his graceless ease at the first halting-place without thought of crowning his progress.

Was Nietzsche actually the first to formulate this question? I dare not affirm that he was, for I am confident he had already come across the problem amongst the Greeks and amongst the Italians of the Renaissance. But with the latter the question was answered immediately, and man turned eagerly to the domain of practical activity. The solution was sought and found unerringly in action and in the practice of the arts. I have in mind Alessandro and Cesare Borgia, Frederick II, King of the Two Sicilies, Leonardo da Vinci, and Goethe—creators, men of a superior race. For artists and for men of action the problem of the *superman* does not exist, or is at least readily solved. Their very lives and activity provide an answer in themselves. The torturing dread begins when the problem is left unsolved, or when the interval between question and answer is protracted. The being, who thinks and invents and does not act, brews his own poison draught. Hearken again to William Blake: *"He who desires but acts not, breeds pestilence"*—the pestilence that proved mortal to Nietzsche.

"What can a man accomplish?" is the atheist's characteristic query, and Dostoevsky exquisitely realized the fact that to deny God is inevitably to exalt man.

God a myth? . . . Then everything is lawful! We find this idea in *The Possessed* and it is repeated in *The Karamazovs*:

"If God exists, all is His will, and from His will I cannot escape. If not, it's all my will and I am bound to show self-will."[1] How can a man assert his independence? Again begins that torturing dread. Everything is possible. Is it? Everything? What can one man accomplish?

Whenever we see one of Dostoevsky's characters ask himself this question, we can be sure of witnessing ere long his utter downfall. Take Raskolnikov, for instance, the first of them to formulate the idea clearly, the very idea which Nietzsche transformed into his theory of the *superman*. Raskolnikov is responsible for an article somewhat subversive in tone, dividing, according to Porfiry's version of it, all men into *ordinary* and *extraordinary*.

"Ordinary men have to live in submission, have no right

[1] *The Possessed*, p. 580.

to transgress the law, because, don't you see, they are ordinary. But extraordinary men have a right to commit any crime and to transgress the law in any way, just because they are extraordinary."—"That wasn't quite my conclusion," began Raskolnikov, simply and modestly. "Yet I admit that you have stated it almost correctly; perhaps, if you like, perfectly so." (It almost gave him pleasure to admit this.) "The only difference is that I don't contend that extra-ordinary people are always bound to commit breaches of morals, as you call it. In fact, I doubt whether such an argu-ment could be published. I simply hinted than an 'extra-ordinary' man has the right . . . that is, not an official right but an inner right to decide in his own conscience to over-step certain obstacles, and only in case it is essential for the practical fulfilment of his idea (sometimes, perhaps, of bene-fit to the whole of humanity). . . . Then, I remember, I main-tain in my article that all—well, legislators and leaders of men, such as Lycurgus, Solon, Mahomet, Napoleon, and so on—were all without exception criminals, from the very fact that, making a new law, they transgressed the ancient one, handed down from their ancestors, and held sacred by the people, and they did not stop short at bloodshed either, if that bloodshed (often of innocent persons fighting bravely in defence of ancient law) were of use to their cause. It's remarkable, in fact, that the majority, indeed, of those bene-factors and leaders of humanity were guilty of terrible carnage. In short, I maintain that all great men, or even a little out of the common, that is to say capable of giving some new word, must from their very nature be criminals —more or less, or course. Otherwise, it's hard for them to get out of the common rut; and to remain in the common rut is what they can't submit to, from their very nature again, and to my mind they ought not, indeed, to submit to it."[1]

[1] *Crime and Punishment*, pp. 236, 237.

Observe, however, that in the face of this profession Raskolnikov confesses his abiding faith in God—a testimony which differentiates him from Dostoevsky's other *supermen*.

"Do you believe in God? Excuse my curiosity!"

"I do," repeated Raskolnikov, raising his eyes to Porfiry.

"And do you—believe in Lazarus's rising from the dead?"

"I do! Why do you ask all this?"

"You believe it literally?"

"Literally."[1]

"One law for the Lion and Ox is Oppression," says William Blake.

But the very fact that Raskolnikov puts himself the question, instead of making action his answer, proves that he is no real *superman*. His bankruptcy is complete. Not for one moment can he rid himself of the conviction of his own mediocrity. He excites himself to commit a crime in order to satisfy himself that he is a *superman*. "I divined then . . . that power is only vouchsafed to the man who dares to stoop and pick it up. There is only one thing, one thing needful: one has only to dare! Then for the first time in my life an idea took shape in my mind which no one had ever thought of before me, not one! I saw as clear as daylight how strange it is that not a single person living in this mad world has had the daring to go straight for it all and send it flying to the devil. I wanted *to have the daring* . . . and I killed her. I only wanted to have the daring."[2]

Later, after the crime, he says: "Perhaps I should never have committed a murder again. I wanted to find out something else; it was something led me on. I wanted to find out then, and quickly, whether I was a louse like everybody else or a man, whether I can step over barriers or not, whether

---

[1] *Crime and Punishment*, p. 238.   [2] *Ibid.*, p. 377.

I dare to stoop to pick up or not, whether I am a trembling creature or whether I have the right. . . ."[1]

Moreover he is unwilling to accept the idea of his own failure. He refuses to acknowledge he had not the right to dare.

"I couldn't carry out even the first step, because I am contemptible, that's what's the matter! . . . If I had succeeded I should have been crowned with glory, but now I'm trapped."[2]

After Raskolnikov, Stavrogin and Kirillov, Ivan Karamazov and the *Raw Youth* will have their turn.

The utter inefficiency of every one of his intellectual heroes is rooted in Dostoevsky's belief that the man of active brain is wellnigh incapable of action.

Notes from Underground, the little book he wrote shortly before *The Eternal Husband*, marks for me the height of his career. It is the keystone of his whole work, the clue to his thought. "*He who thinks, acts not. . . .*" 'Tis but a step then to the insinuation that action presupposes a certain intellectual inferiority.

From first page to last, this little volume, *Notes from Underground*, is a monologue pure and simple, and it really seems a trifle daring to assert, as did our friend Valery Larbaud recently, that James Joyce, the author of *Ulysses*, devised this form of narrative. Had he forgotten Dostoevsky, Poe even, and Browning, of whom I cannot help but think as I read these *Notes from Underground* anew? Browning and Dostoevsky seem to me to bring the monologue straightway to perfection, in all the diversity and subtlety to which this literary form lends itself.

Perhaps I shock the literary sense of some of my audience by coupling these two names, but I can do no other, nor help being struck by the profound resemblance, not merely in form,

[1] *Crime and Punishment*, p. 378.   [2] *Ibid.*, p. 467.

but in substance between certain Browning monologues (I am thinking especially of *My Last Duchess, Porphyria's Lover*, and the two depositions of Pompilia's husband in the *Ring and the Book*) and that admirable little story in Dostoevsky's *Journal, Krotchkaya*, which means, I am told, *Faint Heart*, the title it bears in the latest edition of the volume.

But to an even greater degree than the form and the manner of their work, what urges my comparison of Browning and Dostoevsky is their optimism—an optimism which has no affinity with Goethe's, but brings them both very close to Nietzsche and to William Blake, of whom I shall have occasion to speak again.

Yes, Nietzsche, Dostoevsky, Browning, and Blake, are four stars of one single constellation. For long Blake was completely unknown to me, then recently I discovered him, and as an astronomer can sense the influence of a star and determine its position before he has even glimpsed it, I can say that Blake I had long anticipated. Is this equivalent to saying his influence was considerable? No, indeed! I am not aware he ever exerted any. Even in England, till later years, Blake remained practically unknown, a pure and distant star whose rays are only now reaching us.

The most significant of his works, *The Marriage of Heaven and Hell*, from which I shall quote passages now and again, will help us, I am sure, to a better understanding of certain traits in Dostoevsky.

That sentence I quoted a moment ago from his *Proverbs of Hell*, as he entitles some of his aphorisms, would be a fitting device to introduce Dostoevsky's *Notes from Underground*—or else this other saying of Blake's—"*Expect poison from standing water.*"

"Yes, a man in the nineteenth century must and morally ought to be pre-eminently a characterless creature," declares the hero (save the mark!) of the *Underground*. The man of action according to Dostoevsky must be mediocre in intellect, for the proud in mind are withheld from action which they deem a compromise, a limitation to thought. He who acts will be a Pyotr Stepanovitch, as in *The Possessed*, or a Smerdiakov, for in *Crime and Punishment* Dostoevsky had not yet established the division between thought and action.

The mind does not act; it conditions action. In several of Dostoevsky's novels we come across an odd distribution of rôles, the uneasy relationship and hidden connivance between a thinking being and another acting under its influence, vicariously almost. Think of Ivan Karamazov, Smerdiakov, Stavrogin, and Pyotr Stepanovitch, whom Stavrogin called his "shadow".

Strange, is it not, to find what I may term a first version of the queer relationship between Ivan Karamazov the thinker and Smerdiakov the lackey in *Crime and Punishment*, the first of his great novels? Dostoevsky tells us of one Filka, a serf, Svidrigaïlov's servant, who hanged himself to escape, not blows, but his master's mockery of him. "Filka was a sort of hypochondriac, a sort of domestic philosopher." The other servants used to say "he read himself silly."[1]

These lackeys, these shadows, these puppets that act in place of thinking beings, have one and all a love amounting to veritable devotion for the diabolical superiority of intellect. Stavrogin's prestige in the eyes of Pyotr Stepanovitch is as exaggerated as that intellectual's scorn for his miserable inferior.

" 'Do you want the whole truth?' said Pyotr Stepanovitch to Stavrogin. 'You see the idea really did cross my mind— you hinted at it yourself, not seriously, but teasing me (for of course you would not hint it seriously); but I couldn't bring

[1] *Crime and Punishment*, p. 272.

myself to it, and wouldn't bring myself to it for anything, not for a hundred roubles. . . .'

"In the heat of his talk, he went close up to Stavrogin and took hold of the revers of his coat (really, it may have been on purpose). With a violent movement Stavrogin struck him on the arm: 'Come, what is it? . . . give over, you'll break my arm.' "[1] (Ivan Karamazov's conduct towards Smerdiakov is marked by like brutality.)

"Nicolay Vsyevolodovitch, tell me, as before God, are you guilty or not, and I'll swear I'll believe your word as though it were God's, and I'll follow you to the end of the earth. Yes, I will, I'll follow you like a dog. . . . I am a buffoon, but I don't want you, my better half, to be one! Do you understand me?"[2]

The thinking being enjoys his domination of the other: yet this very domination is a source of constant exasperation. For his creature's fumbling actions are served up as the caricature of his own thoughts.

Dostoevsky's letters enlighten us concerning the elaboration of his novels, *The Possessed* in particular. Personally, I judge this work to be most extraordinarily powerful and wonderful. In it we are vouchsafed to witness a rare literary phenomenon. The book Dostoevsky planned to write was very different from that we actually have. While he was putting it into shape a new character, of which at first he had scarcely dreamed, asserted itself, gradually took front rank, and ousted the intended hero!

"None of my works has given me so much trouble as this one," he wrote from Dresden to his friend Strakhov in October, 1870. "At the beginning, that is, at the end of last year, I thought the novel *made* and artificial, and rather scorned it. But later I was overtaken by real enthusiasm. I fell in love with my work of a sudden and made a big

---

[1] *The Possessed*, pp. 492, 493.   [2] *Ibid.*, pp. 498, 499.

effort to get all that I had written into good trim. Then in the summer came a transformation, up started a new, vital character, who insisted on being the hero of the book, the original hero (a most interesting figure, but not worthy to be called a hero) fell into the background. The new one so inspired me that I once more began to go over the whole book afresh."[1]

The new character, to which all his attention is now devoted, is Stavrogin, the strangest perhaps and the most terrifying of Dostoevsky's creations. Stavrogin reads his own riddle towards the end of the book. It is seldom that a character of Dostoevsky's fails to give, sooner of later, the key, as it were, to his nature, often in most unexpected fashion, by some words he lets slip all of a sudden. Listen, for instance, to Stavrogin's account of himself:

"I have no ties in Russia—everything is as alien to me there as everywhere. It's true that I dislike living there more than anywhere, but I can't hate anything even there! I've tried my strength everywhere. You advised me to do this, 'that I might learn to know myself.' As long as I was experimenting for myself and for others, it seemed infinite, as it has all my life. Before your eyes I endured a blow from your brother; I acknowledged my marriage in public. But to what to apply my strength, that is what I've never seen, and do not see now in spite of all your praises in Switzerland, which I believed in. I am still capable, as I always was, of desiring to do something good, and of feeling pleasure from it; at the same time, I desire evil and feel pleasure from that too."[2]

At our last meeting we shall come back to the first item in this declaration—a very important one in Dostoevsky's estimation. Stavrogin had no ties in his native land. To-day let us consider only this double-headed hydra of desire that

[1] Mayne, p. 198. Letter to N. N. Strakhov, Dresden, October 9, 1870.
[2] *The Possessed*, pp. 634, 635.

is gnawing Stavrogin. Man ever entreats, says Baudelaire, God and the Devil at one and the same time.

At the bottom, what Stavrogin worships is energy. William Blake will give us the key to this baffling character: "*Energy is the only Life—Energy is Eternal Delight.*" Aye, hearken further to his proverbs: "*The road of excess leads to the palace of wisdom,*" or "*If the fool would persist in his folly he would become wise.*"—"*You never know what is enough unless you know what is more than enough.*" Blake's glorification of energy expresses itself in divers forms. "*The roaring of lions, the howling of wolves, the raging of the stormy sea, and the destructive sword are portions of eternity too great for the eye of man.*"

We further read: "*The cistern contains: the fountain overflows,*" and "*The tigers of wrath are wiser than the horses of instruction.*" And the formula which introduces his *Marriage of Heaven and Hell* seems to have been appropriated all unconsciously by Dostoevsky: "*Without Contraries is no progression. Attraction and Repulsion, Reason and Energy, Love and Hate, are necessary to human existence.*" "*These two classes of men are always upon earth, and they shall be enemies: whoever tries to reconcile them seeks to destroy existence.*"

Allow me to add to Blake's proverbs two of my own invention: "*Fine feelings are the stuff that bad literature is made on,*" and "*The Fiend is a party to every work of art.*" Yes, of a truth, every work of art is a *Marriage of Heaven and Hell*, and William Blake tells us: "*The reason Milton wrote in fetters when he wrote of Angels and God, and at liberty when of Devils and Hell, is because he was a true Poet, and of the Devil's party without knowing it.*"

Dostoevsky was tormented his life long by his horror of evil and by his sense of its inevitability. By evil I mean suffering also. I think of him when I read the parable of the man which sowed good seed in his field, but while men slept his enemy came and sowed tares among the wheat, and went his

way. But when the blade was sprung up, and brought forth
fruit, then appeared the tares also. . . . And the servants said
unto him, Wilt thou then that we go and gather them up?
But he said, Nay: lest while ye gather up the tares, ye root up
also the wheat with them. Let them both grow together until
the harvest.

Two years ago, in neutral territory, I met Walther
Rathenau. He spent two days with me, I remember, and
I questioned him on the events of the time, seeking in particular his opinion of Bolshevism and the Russian Revolution. His answer was that naturally he suffered at the
horrible abominations practised by the revolutionaries.
"But, believe me," he added, "a nation learns to know itself,
as a man his own soul, only by passing through the depths of
suffering and the abyss of sin. . . . And America has not yet
gained a soul because she refuses to accept sin and suffering."

Now you know my grounds for saying, when we saw
Father Zossima kneel before Dmitri, and Raskolnikov before Sonia, that they were humbling themselves, not
merely before suffering, but before sin.

Let us make no mistake as regards what was in
Dostoevsky's mind. I repeat that even though he clearly
formulates the problem of the *superman* which insidiously
reappears in each of his works, we witness the glorious
vindication of none but Gospel truths. Dostoevsky per-
ceives and imagines salvation only in the individual's
renunciation of self; but, on the other hand, he gives us to
understand that man is never nearer God than in his
extremity of anguish. Then and not till then does he cry:
"*Lord, to whom shall we go? Thou hast the words of eternal life.*"

He knows this imploring cry cannot proceed from the lips
of the righteous man who has ever been sure of his course
and confident he has acquitted his obligations to God and to
himself alike, but from those of the unhappy creature "who

has nowhere left to turn." . . . "Do you understand what it means when you have absolutely nowhere to turn? No, that you don't understand yet!"[1] Only through anguish and crime, after his expiation even, cut off from the society of his fellow-men, did Raskolnikov come face to face with the Gospel.

There has no doubt been a measure of desultoriness in the ideas I have submitted to you to-day—but maybe responsibility for the confusion falls in part to Dostoevsky's share as well. *"Improvement makes straight roads; but the crooked roads without improvement are roads of Genius."*

At all events, Dostoevsky was convinced, as I too am convinced, that in the Gospel truths is no confusion—the one consideration of moment!

[1] *Crime and Punishment*, p. 14.

VI

I AM overwhelmed by the number and importance of the things I have still left to say to you. You have grasped, have you not, what I meant in my introduction when I said that Dostoevsky was often an excuse for expressing my own ideas? I should crave your pardon did I think that thereby I had presented Dostoevsky's in a false light. No, like the bees Montaigne tells of, I have but gathered from his works what I needed to make my own honey. However life-like a portrait, there is always much of the artist in it, as much of him almost as of the sitter. The most precious model is undoubtedly that which warrants the widest diversity of likeness and lends itself to the greatest number of portraits. I have attempted Dostoevsky's likeness; I know I have not exhausted his semblance.

Overwhelming, too, the number of touches I should like to add to my preceding papers. After each one I have felt there was something I had forgotten to tell you. At our last meeting, for example, I wanted to make plain the meaning of my two "proverbs": *"Fine feelings are the stuff bad literature is made on,"* and *"The Fiend is party to every work of art."* What to me seems transparent may appear a paradox to you, and as such to call for elucidation. I loathe paradoxes and never seek effect in surprises, but had I nothing new to suggest I should not attempt these papers; and remember, a new idea wears invariably the guise of a paradox. To help you acknowledge the truth of what I am saying, I proposed to call your attention to two figures, St. Francis of Assisi and Fra Angelico. If it was vouchsafed the latter to be a great artist (the better to prove my contention I choose as my example the most shiningly pure figure in the whole history of art), it was because, in spite of his purity, his art permitted of demonic collaboration. There is no work of art to which the Demon is not a co-signatory. The true saint is not Fra Angelico, but Francis of Assisi. There are no artists amongst the saints, no saints amongst the artists.

Creative art may be likened to the box of sweet spices which Mary Magdalene brake not. I have already quoted that strange dictum of Blake's: *"The reason Milton wrote in fetters when he wrote of Angels and God, and at liberty when of Devils and Hell, is because he was a true Poet and of the Devil's party without knowing it."*

There are three threads in the loom on which every work of art is woven, the three lusts pointed out by the apostle: *". . . the lust of the flesh, and the lust of the eyes, and the pride of life."*

Remember Lacordaire's remark when congratulated upon an admirable sermon he had just delivered: "The Devil has forestalled you." The Devil would not have told him his sermon was fine, indeed, he would have been there to speak, had he not been party to it.

After citing lines from Schiller's *Hymn to Joy*, Dmitri Karamazov exclaims: "And the awful thing is that beauty is mysterious as well as terrible. God and the Devil are fighting there and the battlefield is the heart of man."[1]

No artist, I am sure, has given the demonic so large a share in his work as Dostoevsky, unless Blake himself, who concluded his admirable little book, *The Marriage of Heaven and Hell*, with these words:

"This Angel who is now become a Devil is my particular friend. We often read the Bible together in its infernal or diabolical sense, which the world shall have if they behave well."

After leaving you, I realized that in quoting the strangest of William Blake's *Proverbs of Hell*, I had omitted to read to

[1] *The Brothers Karamazov*, p. 110.

you the entire passage from *The Possessed* which had called
forth these very quotations. May I atone for my omission?
In this one page from *The Possessed* you will marvel at the
fusion—not to say confusion—of the divers elements
I sought to point out in my previous papers: optimism first
and foremost, the wild love of life we come across again and
again in Dostoevsky's works, love of life and all the world,
Blake's vast delectable world wherein dwells the tiger as well
as the lamb.

"Are you fond of children?"

"I am," answered Kirillov, though rather indifferently.

"Then you're fond of life?"

"Yes, I'm fond of life! What of it?"

"Though you've made up your mind to shoot yourself?"

"What of it? Why connect it? Life's one thing, and that's
another. Life exists, but death doesn't at all. . . ."[1]

We saw too Dmitri Karamazov ready to take his life in a
fit of optimism, beside himself with enthusiasm.

"You seem to be very happy, Kirillov?"

"Yes, very happy," he answered, as though making the
ordinary reply.

"But you were distressed so lately, angry with Liputin?"

"H'm! . . . I'm not scolding now. I did not know then that
I was happy."[2]

Do not draw a mistaken conclusion from this seeming
ferocity which is frequent in Dostoevsky. It is an integral
part of his quietism, as of Blake's. You remember my saying
that Dostoevsky's Christianity had closer affinities with Asia
than with Rome? Yet his acceptance of the doctrine of
energy, a doctrine positively glorified by Blake, is rather of
the West than of the East.

But for Blake and Dostoevsky both, the truth of New
Testament teaching is too radiantly clear for them to deny

[1] *The Possessed*, p. 219.   [2] *Ibid.*, p. 220.

this ferocity as but a transitory phase, the short-lived consequence of a passing blindness.

And to reveal to you only the vision of his cruelty would be an act of treachery towards Blake. I wish I could counter my quotations from his terrible *Proverbs of Hell* by reading one of the loveliest of his *Songs of Innocence*—alas! its aëry form eludes translation—the poem where he foretells the time when the lion in his strength will lie down with the lamb and watch over the fold.

But let us continue with our reading from *The Possessed.*

"They're bad because they don't know they're good; when they find out they won't outrage a little girl. They'll find out that they're good and they'll all become good, every one of them," declares Kirillov.[1]

And so the conversation continues until we stumble across the singular conception of the man-God.

"Here you've found it out! So you've become good then?"

"I am good."

"That I agree with, though," muttered Stavrogin, frowning.

"He who teaches that all are good will end the world."

"He who taught it was crucified."

"He will come, and his name will be the man-God."

"The God-man?"

"The man-God! That's the difference."[2]

The notion of a man-God succeeding the God-man brings us round again to Nietzsche. À propos of the *superman* theory, I should like to contribute one emendation in protest against an opinion which is only too current and too easily accepted. Nietzsche's *superman* (observe, pray, wherein he differs from the *superman* of Raskolnikov's or Kirillov's vision), though *ruthlessness* is his motto, is ruthless not to

[1] *The Possessed*, p. 221.   [2] *Ibid.*, p. 221.

others but to himself. The humanity he aspires to outstrip is his own. In short: to one and the same problem Nietzsche and Dostoevsky propose different, radically opposed solutions. Nietzsche advocates the affirmation of the personality —for him it is the one possible aim in life: Dostoevsky postulates its surrender. Nietzsche presupposes the heights of achievement where Dostoevsky prophesies utter ruin.

At the darkest hour of the War, I read in the letters of a Red Cross orderly (his modesty forbids me to name him), living in the midst of agonizing sufferings and hearing but the voice of despair, "Ah, if only they could make a sacrifice of their sufferings!"—a thought so luminous that all commentary were a matter for reproach. I shall only compare it with this sentence from *The Possessed*:

"Every earthly woe and every earthly tear is a joy for us. And when you water the earth with your tears a foot deep, you will rejoice at everything at once, and your sorrow will be no more, such is the prophecy."[1] Are not we very near to Pascal's *"sweet and perfect resignation"* and his cry of *"Joy! Joy! Tears of joy!"*?

Is not this state of bliss depicted by Dostoevsky the very one exalted by the Gospel, a state into which we are born anew, the joy whose fulfilment is possible only through renunciation of self, for it is love of self which prevents us from leaping into Eternity, from entering into the Kingdom of God and communing in the mystery of life universal?

The first consequence of such regeneration is that man becomes as a little child. *"Except ye be converted, and become as little children, ye shall not enter into the Kingdom of Heaven."* In the words of La Bruyère, *"Little children have neither past nor future, for they live in the present,"* which man has lost the power to do.

"At that moment," said Prince Myshkin to Rogozhin—

[1] *The Possessed*, p. 133.

"at that moment I seem somehow to understand the extra-ordinary saying that *there shall be no more time.*"[1]

This direct participation is, as I have earlier indicated, taught by the Gospel, unwearying in its insistence upon these words, "*Et nunc*" . . . "*And now.*" The perfect joy Christ means is not of the future, but of the immediate present.

"You've begun to believe in future eternal life?"

"No, not in a future eternal life, but in eternal life here. There are moments, you reach moments, and time suddenly stands still and it will become eternal."[2]

And towards the end of *The Possessed* Dostoevsky reverts once more to Kirillov's uncanny rapture. Let us read the passage in question. It will help us to appreciate Dostoevsky's idea, and prepare the way for one of the most essential truths I have left to discuss.

"There are seconds—they come five or six at a time—when you suddenly feel the presence of the eternal harmony perfectly attained. It's something not earthly—I don't mean in the sense that it's heavenly—but in that sense that man cannot endure it in his earthly aspect. He must be physically changed or die. This feeling is clear and unmistakable; it's as though you apprehend all nature and suddenly say, 'Yes, that's right.' God, when He created the world, said at the end of each day of creation, 'Yes, it's right, it's good.' It—it's not being deeply moved, but simply joy. You don't forgive anything, because there is no more need of forgiveness. It's not that you love—oh, there's something in it higher than love—what's most awful is that it's terribly clear and such joy. If it lasted more than five seconds, the soul could not endure it and must perish. In those five seconds I live through a lifetime, and I'd give my whole life for them, because they are worth it. To endure ten seconds one must

[1] *The Idiot*, p. 225. [2] *The Possessed*, p. 219.

be physically changed. I think man ought to give up having children—what's the use of children, what's the use of evolution when the goal has been attained? In the Gospel it is written that there will be no child-bearing in the resurrection, but that man will be like the angels of the Lord. . . ."[1]

" 'Kirillov, does this often happen?'

" 'Once in three days, or once a week.'

" 'Don't you have fits, perhaps?'

" 'No.'

" 'Well, you will. Be careful, Kirillov. I've heard that's just how fits begin. An epileptic described exactly that sensation before a fit, word for word as you've done. He mentioned five seconds too, and said that more could not be endured. Remember Mahomet's pitcher from which no drop of water was spilt while he circled Paradise on his horse. That was a case of five seconds too; that's too much like your eternal harmony, and Mahomet was an epileptic. Be careful, Kirillov, it's epilepsy.'

" 'It won't have time.' Kirillov smiled gently."[2]

In *The Idiot* we hear Prince Myshkin connect this condition of euphoria, familiar to him too, with the epileptic attacks to which he is subject.

So there we have Prince Myshkin an epileptic, Kirillov an epileptic, Smerdiakov an epileptic. There is an epileptic in each of Dostoevsky's great works. We know Dostoevsky himself was thus afflicted, and his persistence in making epilepsy intervene as a factor in his novels sufficiently indicates the rôle he assigned this disease in moulding his ethical conceptions and directing the course of his thought.

If we seek far enough, we shall invariably find the genesis of every serious moral reform in some physiological enigma, some non-satisfaction of the flesh, irritation, or anomaly.

[1] *The Possessed*, pp. 554–5.   [2] *Ibid.*, p. 555.

Forgive me for quoting myself again, but if I am to express my idea as explicitly as before, I must use the same phraseology as on that previous occasion.

"It is natural that every important moral change, or, as Nietzsche would say, *transmutation of values*, should be due to some physiological disturbance. With physical well-being, mental activity is in abeyance, and as long as conditions continue to be satisfactory, no change can possibly be contemplated. By conditions I mean spiritual circumstance, for where the external and material are implicated, the reformer's motive is utterly different; the one readjustment involved is chemical, the other mechanical. There lies at the root of every reform a distemper. The reformer is a sick man by reason of some ill-adjustment in his spiritual balance. Densities, ratios, and moral values present themselves to him in different perspectives, so he exerts himself to establish a fresh accord. He aims at a new co-ordination. His work is nothing but an attempt to reorganize, in the light of his logic and reasoning, the elements of confusion he senses within himself, for the unsystematic he cannot tolerate. Of course I do not suggest that lack of balance is the necessary condition for the making of a reformer, but I do contend that every reformer starts out with a lack of balance."[1]

So far as I know, it would be impossible to find, amongst the reformers who have held up to humanity a new measure of values, one single instance where we could fail to discern what Dr. Binet-Sanglé is pleased to qualify a *hereditary taint*.[2]

Mahomet was an epileptic. Epileptics, too, the Prophets of Israel, and Luther, and Dostoevsky. Socrates had his demon,

[1] André Gide, *Morceaux Choisis*, p. 101, §1.

[2] Dr. Binet-Sanglé is the author of a blasphemous work to which he has given the title *La Folie de Jésus-Christ*: he attempts to deny the importance of Christ and of Christianity by showing that Christ was mad and a degenerate.

Saint Paul his mysterious "thorn in the flesh", Pascal his abyss, Nietzsche and Rousseau their mania.

I can hear you say, "But what is there new in this theory? It belongs properly to Lombroso and Max Nordau. Genius is a neurosis." No, not so fast! I must insist on this point, for it is extraordinarily important.

There do exist geniuses, Victor Hugo for example, sane and whole. Their perfect spiritual poise precludes the possibility of any fresh problem. Rousseau, without his leaven of madness, would, I am sure, be no better than an undigested Cicero. It is pointless to lament the infirmity but for which he would never have sought to analyse the problem raised by his own anomaly or find a harmony which would not reject his discord. Sound and healthy reformers do undoubtedly exist, but such are law-givers. The man whose inner balance is perfect can well contribute reforms—reforms which touch the outer man: he draws up new constitutions. But the individual who is abnormal refuses to submit to laws already established.

From knowledge of his own case, Dostoevsky supposes a pathological condition which, for a space, imposes and suggests to one or other of his characters a new formula of existence. To take a concrete instance, let us consider Kirillov, who carries on his shoulders the entire plot of *The Possessed*. We are aware that he intends to take his life, but not that his suicide is imminent: self-destruction is, however, certainly in his mind. Why? The motive is withheld almost till the very end of the book.

"I don't understand what fancy possesses you to put yourself to death," says Pyotr Stepanovitch to him. "It wasn't my idea; you thought of it yourself before I appeared, and talked of your intention to the committee abroad before you said anything to me. And you know, no one has forced it on you; no one of them knew you, but you came to confide in them yourself, from sentimentalism. And what's to be done if a plan of action here, which can't be altered now, was founded upon that with your consent and upon your suggestion?—*your* suggestion, mind that!"[1]

Kirillov's suicide is absolutely gratuitous. I mean to say there is an absence of outward motivation. We shall presently see what absurdities are introduced into this world under cover of a *gratuitous act*.

After Kirillov resolves to take his life, everything becomes a matter of profound indifference to him. His peculiar state of mind which sanctions and accounts for his suicide (gratuitous, but *not* without a motive) will leave him unmoved by the imputation of a crime others will commit and which he will calmly suffer to be laid at his own door. Such at least is Pyotr Stepanovitch's belief.

Pyotr Stepanovitch imagines the crime he is planning will strengthen the bonds between the conspirators he heads and over whom he feels his control weakening. He reckons that each individual party to the plot, having shared in the crime, will feel his complicity and be unable, indeed will not dare, to break away. Who is to be sacrificed?

Pyotr Stepanovitch is still undecided. It is necessary that the victim should present himself spontaneously.

The conspirators are met together in a large room; in the course of conversation, the question is asked, "Can there be, even now, an informer in our midst?" An extraordinary commotion follows this remark: everybody begins to talk at once.

" 'Gentlemen, if that is so,' Verhovensky went on, 'I have compromised myself more than anyone, and so I will ask you to answer one question, if you care to, of course. You are all perfectly free.'

" 'What question? What question?' everyone clamoured.

[1] *The Possessed*, p. 577.

" 'A question that will make it clear whether we are to remain together, or take up our hats and go our several ways without speaking.'

" 'The question! The question!'

" 'If any one of us knew of a proposed political murder, would he, in view of the consequences, go to give information, or would he stay at home and await events? Opinions may differ on this point. The answer to the question will tell us clearly whether we are to separate, or to remain together, and for far longer than this one evening.'

"After which Pyotr Stepanovitch begins to interrogate apart several members of this secret society. He is interrupted.

" 'It's an unnecessary question. Everyone will make the same answer. There are no informers here.'

" 'What's that gentleman getting up for?' cried the girl student.

" 'That's Shatov. What are you getting up for?' cried the lady of the house.

"Shatov did, in fact, stand up. He was holding his cap in his hand and looking at Verhovensky. Apparently he wanted to say something to him, but was hesitating. His face was pale and wrathful, but he controlled himself. He did not say one word, but in silence walked towards the door.

" 'Shatov, this won't make things better for you!' Verhovensky called after him enigmatically.

" 'But it will for you, since you are a spy and a scoundrel!' Shatov shouted to him from the door as he went out.

"Shouts and exclamations again.

" 'That's what comes of a test,' cried a voice."[1]

Thus the victim is marked, and by his own hand. Haste is imperative: Shatov's murder must anticipate his denunciation.

[1] *The Possessed*, pp. 383, 385.

We must admire Dostoevsky's art in this, because constantly carried away in my enthusiasm to discuss his ideas, I am afraid I have neglected all too much his wonderful skill in exposition.

At this juncture in the narrative, an astounding thing comes to pass which raises a particular artistic problem. It is a commonplace that, passed a certain point in the evolution of the plot, there must be nothing to deflect attention: events must move more quickly and lead straight to the ultimate issue. Well, this is the moment, when the action has entered on its phase of maximum rapidity, that Dostoevsky contrives to introduce the most startling interruptions. He is conscious that, so tense is his reader's attention, everything will assume an importance out of all proportion. With this knowledge, he does not hesitate to distract attention from the main course of events by brusque modulations which develop his most cherished ideas. The very night Shatov is destined to turn informer or be murdered, his wife, whom he has not seen for years, suddenly reappears at his house. Her time is at hand, but at first Kirillov does not realize her condition.

Inadequately handled, this scene could become grotesque. It ranks amongst the finest in the book. In theatrical jargon it would be described as a *utility*, in literature as a *cheville*, but it is precisely one of the rarest manifestations of Dostoevsky's artistry. Like Pushkin he could say, "I have never treated anything lightly," which is the hallmark of a great artist, utilizing everything, transforming disadvantage into opportunity. At this stage the pace needs must slacken, and every detail that can arrest events in their precipitancy becomes of supreme importance. The passages where Dostoevsky describes the arrival, unannounced, of Shatov's wife, the conversation between husband and wife, Kirillov's interposition, and the prompt establishment of an intimacy between the two men, constitute perhaps the most moving chapter in the book. We marvel anew at the utter absence of jealousy I discussed with you on a previous occasion. Shatov knows that his wife is going to have a child, but the father of this child she expects is not even mentioned. Shatov is consumed with love for this suffering creature who can find none but words that wound.

"It was only that fact [i.e. his wife's reappearance] that saved the scoundrels from Shatov's carrying out his intention, and at the same time helped them to get rid of him. To begin with, it agitated Shatov, threw him out of his regular routine, and deprived him of his usual clear-sightedness and caution. Any idea of his own danger would be the last thing to enter his head at this moment when he was absorbed with such different considerations."[1]

But to come back to Kirillov; the time is at hand when Pyotr Stepanovitch calculates personal advantage from the other man's suicide. What grounds has Kirillov for taking his own life? Pyotr Stepanovitch questions him: he has no clear idea, and is seeking clumsily to get at the truth. Up till the last minute, he is in terror lest Kirillov change his mind and thus escape him. But no!

"I won't put it off. I want to kill myself now,"[2] says Kirillov.

The conversation between Verhovensky and Kirillov is especially obscure, obscure even in Dostoevsky's own mind. As we have earlier observed, Dostoevsky never expresses his ideas as ideas pure and simple, but always through the medium of his characters who become their interpreters. Kirillov is in a highly unusual pathological state, for in a moment or two he is going to take his own life, and his talk is agitated and incoherent. We are left to unravel in it the clue to Dostoevsky's own thought.

[1] *The Possessed*, p. 540.   [2] *Ibid.*, p. 275.

The idea which prompts Kirillov's suicide is of a mystic nature and closed to Pyotr Stepanovitch's comprehension.

"If God exists, all is His will, and from His will I cannot escape. If not, it's all my will, and I am bound to show self-will. . . . I am bound to show myself because the highest point of my self-will is to kill myself with my own hands. . . ."

" 'God is necessary and so must exist,' said Kirillov.

" 'Well, that's all right then,' encouraged Pyotr Stepanovitch.

" 'But I know He doesn't and can't.'

" 'That's more likely.'

" 'Surely you must understand that a man with two such ideas can't go on living?'

" 'Must shoot himself, you mean?'

" 'Surely you understand that one might shoot oneself for that alone?'

" 'But you won't be the only one to kill yourself: there are lots of suicides.'

" 'With good cause! But to do it without any cause at all, simply for self-will, I am the only one.'

" 'He won't shoot himself,' flashed across Pyotr Stepanovitch's mind again.

" 'Do you know,' he observed irritably, 'if I were in your place, I should kill someone else to show my self-will, not myself. You might be of use. I'll tell you whom, if you are not afraid. Then you needn't shoot yourself to-day, perhaps. We may come to terms.' "[1]

For a moment Pyotr Stepanovitch dreams, in the event of Kirillov's refusing to carry out his plan of self-destruction, of using him as the instrument to murder Shatov, instead of merely imputing the crime to him.

[1] *The Possessed*, pp. 579, 580.

" 'To kill someone else would be the lowest point of self-will, and you should show your whole soul in that. I am not you; I want the highest point, and I'll kill myself. . . . I am bound to show my unbelief,' said Kirillov, walking about the room. 'I have no higher idea than disbelief in God. I have all the history of mankind on my side. Man has done nothing but invent God so as to go on living, and not kill himself: that's the whole of universal history up till now. I am the first one in the whole history of mankind who would not invent God.' "[1]

Do not forget Dostoevsky's Christianity is real. What he reveals in Kirillov's declaration is again a case of moral bankruptcy. Dostoevsky, I repeat, has visions of salvation only through renunciation. But a fresh idea has crept in to complicate his theory: to illuminate it, I must have recourse once more to William Blake's *Proverbs of Hell*.

"*If others had not been foolish, we should be so.*" In order that we might be spared foolishness, others consented to foolishness before us.

Into Kirillov's half-mad brain enters the idea of sacrifice: "I will begin and open the door and save—mankind."

If it is necessary that Kirillov be abnormal in order to entertain such ideas—ideas moreover which Dostoevsky does not unreservedly sanction since they betoken insubordination—there is none the less a particle of truth in his conception, and if it is necessary that Kirillov be abnormal in order to entertain such ideas, it is that we also may have them in our day, yet be in our right mind.

" 'So at last you understand!' cried Kirillov rapturously. 'So it can be understood if even a fellow like you understands. Do you understand now that salvation for all consists in proving this idea to everyone? Who will prove it? I! I can't understand how an atheist could know that there is

[1] *The Possessed*, p. 580.

no God and not kill himself on the spot. To recognize that
there is no God, and not to recognize at the same instant that
one is God oneself is an absurdity, else one would certainly
kill oneself. If you recognize it, you are sovereign, and then
you won't kill yourself, but live in the greatest glory.
But one, the first, must kill himself, for else who will
begin and prove it? So I must certainly kill myself, to
begin and prove it. Now I am only a God against my
will, and I am unhappy because I am bound to assert my
will. All are unhappy because all are afraid to express their
will. Man has hitherto been so unhappy and so poor because
he has been afraid to assert his will up to the highest point,
and has shown his self-will only in little things, like a
schoolboy. . . . But I will assert my will, I am bound to
believe that I don't believe. I will begin and will make an end
of it and open the door, and save—mankind. For three
years I've been seeking the attribute of my Godhead and I've
found it; the attribute of my Godhead is self-will. That's all
I can do to prove in the highest point my independence and
my new terrible freedom. For it is very terrible, and I am
killing myself to prove my independence and my new
terrible freedom.' "[1]

Blasphemous as Kirillov's words may appear, rest assured
that Dostoevsky, in drawing his figure, was possessed by the
idea of Christ, by the necessity of the Crucifixion as a
sacrifice to redeem mankind. If Christ had to be offered up,
was it not that we, Christians, might be such without
dying His death? *"If Thou be Christ, save Thyself!"* If Christ
had saved Himself, mankind would have been lost: to save
it, He surrendered His own life.

These few lines of Dostoevsky's, taken from his *Essay on
the Bourgeoisie*, throw fresh light on Kirillov's figure.

"Be clear as to my meaning! Voluntary sacrifice, offered

[1] *The Possessea*, pp. 582, 583.

consciously and without constraint, the sacrifice of the individual for the good of mankind, is to my mind the mark of personality in its noblest and highest development, of perfect self-control—the absolute expression of free will. To offer one's life for others, to suffer for others on the cross or at the stake, is possible only when there is a powerful development of the personality. A strongly-developed personality, conscious of its right to be such, having cast out fear, cannot use itself, cannot be used except in sacrifice for others, that these become like unto itself, self-determinate and happy. It is Nature's law, and mankind tends to reach it."[1]

At last you see why behind Kirillov's talk, which seemed at first hearing somewhat incoherent, we succeed in discerning what was the philosophy of Dostoevsky himself.

I am conscious how far I am from having exhausted the teaching that can be found in his books. I insist once more on the fact that I have sought, consciously or unconsciously, what had most intimate connection with my own ideas. Others no doubt will be able to discern different things. And now that I am come to the end of my last paper, you are awaiting, I am sure, a conclusion of some kind from me. Whither does Dostoevsky lead us? What precisely is his teaching?

Some will say that he leads us straight to Bolshevism, although they know the horror Dostoevsky professed for anarchy. The whole of *The Possessed* prophesies the revolution of which Russia is at present in the throes. But every man who, in defiance of existing systems, contributes new *tables of values* is bound to seem, in the eyes of the conservative, an anarchist. Conservative and nationalist, deigning to see no more than what is chaotic in Dostoevsky, conclude he can be of no service whatsoever to us. To which my reply is that their opposition seems to do great hurt to the genius of France. By our unwillingness to accept anything

[1] Bienstock, pp. 540–2.

foreign unless it reflects our system and logic, our whole likeness, in short, we err most grievously. His conception of beauty happens to differ from our Mediterranean standards, and were the divergence even greater, of what use would our national genius be, how could we apply our logic practically, unless in instances which clamour for regulation? In meditating none but her own likeness, the reflection of her past, France is exposed to a mortal danger. Let me explain my meaning as accurately and temperately as possible. It is well that France should have conservative elements reacting and taking stand against what savours of foreign invasion. But what justifies the existence of these elements if not this fresh contribution without which French culture would ere long be nothing but a hollow form. a hardened shell? What do they know of France's genius? What *do* we know, except its past? It is the same with national feeling as with the Church. I mean the conservative elements often mete out to genius the same treatment as the Church to her saints at times. Many who were rejected, repulsed, denied in the name of tradition, are become its very corner-stones.

My opinion of intellectual protectionism I have often voiced: I believe it presents a great peril; on the other hand, any essay in intellectual denationalization involves a risk no less considerable. I am merely expressing what was Dostoevsky's finding likewise. There never was author more Russian in the strictest sense of the word and withal so universally European. Because it is essentially Russian, his humanity is all-embracing and touches each one of us personally.

"Veteran European Russian" he chose to describe himself. I shall let Versilov of *A Raw Youth* develop Dostoevsky's idea this time!

"The highest Russian thought is the reconciliation of ideas, and who in the whole world could understand such a thought at that time? I was a solitary wanderer: I am rot

speaking of myself personally—it's the Russian idea I'm
speaking of. There all was strife and logic; there the Frenchman was nothing but a Frenchman, the German nothing but
a German, and this more intensely so than at any time in
their history. Consequently never had the Frenchman done
so much harm to France, or the German to Germany, as just
at that time! In these days in all Europe there was not one
European! I alone of all the vitriol-throwers could have told
them to their face that their Tuileries was a mistake. And
I alone among the avenging reactionists could have told
them that the Tuileries, although a crime, was none the less
logical. And that, my boy, was because I, as a Russian, was
the only European in Russia. I am not talking of the whole
Russian idea. . . .

"Europe has created a noble type of Frenchman, of
Englishman, and of German, but of the man of the future
she scarcely knows at present. And, I fancy, so far she does
not want to know. And that one can well imagine; they are
not free, and we are free. I, with my Russian melancholy,
was the only one free in Europe. . . . Take note, my dear, of
a strange fact: every Frenchman can serve not only his
France, but humanity, only on condition that he remains
French to the utmost possible degree, and it's the same for
the Englishman and the German. Only to the Russian, even
in our day, has been vouchsafed the capacity to become
most of all Russian only when he is most European, and this
is true even in our day, that is, long before the millennium
has been reached."[1]

But, to offset this declaration and show how acutely conscious Dostoevsky was of the danger to any country in too
marked europeanization, I must read you this remarkable
passage from *The Possessed*:

" 'Science and reason have, from the beginning of time,

[1] *A Raw Youth*, pp. 462–4.

played a secondary and subordinate part in the life of nations; so it will be till the end of time. Nations are built up and moved by another force which sways and dominates them, the origin of which is unknown and inexplicable; that force is the force of an insatiable desire to go on to the end, though at the same time it denies that end. It is the force of persistent assertion of one's own existence, and a denial of death. It's the spirit of life, as the Scriptures call it, the river of living water, the drying up of which is threatened in the Apocalypse. It's the æsthetic principle, as the philosophers call it, the ethical principle with which they identify it, "the seeking for God," as I call it more simply. The object of every national movement, in every people and at every period of its existence, is only the seeking for its God, who must be its own God, and the faith in Him as the only true one. God is the synthetic personality of the whole people, taken from its beginning to its end. It has never happened that all, or even many, peoples have had one common god, but each has always had its own. It's a sign of the decay of nations when they begin to have gods in common. When gods are common to several nations the gods are dying and the faith in them, together with the nations themselves. The stronger a people, the more individual their God. There never has been a nation without a religion, that is, without an idea of good and evil. Every people has its own conception of good and evil, and its own good and evil. When the same conception of good and evil become prevalent in several nations, then these nations are dying, and then the very distinction between good and evil is beginning to disappear.[1] . . . These are your own words, Stavrogin. . . . I haven't altered anything of your ideas, or even of your words, not a syllable.'

[1] Reclus, *Geography*, XIV, 931. "The island populations of Oceania are fast dying out, for they have lost the body of ideas which governed their actions, and lack a common measure to judge good and evil."

" 'I don't agree that you've not altered anything,' Stavrogin observed cautiously. 'You accepted them with ardour, and in your ardour have transformed them unconsciously. The very fact that you reduce God to a simple attribute of nationality. . . .'

"He suddenly began watching Shatov with intense and peculiar attention, not so much his words as himself.

" 'I reduce God to an attribute of nationality?' cried Shatov. 'On the contrary, I raise the people to God. And has it ever been otherwise? The people is the body of God. Every people is only a people so long as it has its own God and excludes all other gods on earth irreconcilably, so long as it believes that by its God it will conquer and drive out of the world all other gods. Such, from the beginning of time, has been the belief of all great nations, all, anyway, who have been specially remarkable, all who have been leaders of humanity. There is no going against facts. The Jews lived only to await the coming of the true God and left the world the true God. The Greeks deified nature and bequeathed the world their religion, that is, philosophy and art. Rome deified the people in the State, and bequeathed the idea of the State to the nations. France throughout her long history was only the incarnation and development of the Roman God....

" 'If a great people does not believe that the truth is only to be found in itself (in itself alone and in it exclusively), if it does not believe it alone is fit and destined to raise up and save all the rest by its truth, it would at once sink into being ethnographical material, and not a great people. A really great people can never accept a secondary part in the history of humanity, nor even one of the first, but will have the first. A nation which loses this belief ceases to be a nation.' "[1]

And by the way of corollary, we have Stavrogin's reflec-

[1] *The Possessed*, pp. 232-4.

tion which might be a fitting conclusion: "An individual out of touch with his country has lost God."

What would Dostoevsky think of Russia to-day and of her people? It is a painful speculation. . . . Did he apprehend, was he able to foresee her ghastly torments?

In *The Possessed* we find all the seeds of Bolshevism. You need only listen to Shigalev's exposition of his theory and the admission he makes at its close:

"I am perplexed by my own data and my conclusion is a direct contradiction to the original idea with which I start. Starting from unlimited freedom, I arrive at unlimited despotism."[1] And that loathsome Pyotr Stepanovitch Verhovensky exults: "There's going to be such an upset as the world has never seen before. . . . Russia will be overwhelmed with darkness, the earth will weep for its old gods."[2]

Imprudent, dishonest even, I admit, to impute to the author himself the thoughts expressed by the characters in his novels or tales. But we know this was Dostoevsky's medium of expression, often utilizing a colourless individual to formulate one of his cherished truths. We seem to hear him speak from the lips of a secondary character in *The Eternal Husband* when the "malady of the age" is mentioned.

"To be a good citizen is better than being in aristocratic society. I say that because in Russia, nowadays, one doesn't know whom to respect. You'll agree that its a serious malady of the age, when people don't know whom to respect, isn't it?"[3]

I am sure that beyond the darkness enveloping tortured Russia to-day Dostoevsky would still see the light of hope. Perhaps too he would think (the idea appears several times in his novels and in his letters) that Russia is offering herself in sacrifice like Kirillov, and for the salvation, perhaps, of the rest of Europe, and of humanity.

---

[1] *The Possessed*, p. 376.   [2] *Ibid.*, p. 395.
[3] *The Eternal Husband*, p. 128.

THE BROTHERS KARAMAZOV

DOSTOEVSKY—"the only person who has taught me anything about psychology," said Nietzsche.

The fortune he has met with at our hands has been a most singular one. De Vogüé, who was the first to introduce Russian literature to France, seemed appalled at the enormity of this monster. He apologized, he smoothly forestalled the bewilderment of the first readers; thanks to him Turgeniev had been warmly appreciated, everyone could admire Pushkin and Gogol without a qualm, Tolstoy was given unbounded credit, but Dostoevsky . . . no, he was really too Russian. De Vogüé urged caution. The most he could bring himself to do was to direct the curiosity of Dostoevsky's first readers to the two or three works which he considered the most accessible and which required the least mental exertion. But, unfortunately, in so doing he dismissed the most significant ones, no doubt the most difficult but also, it is safe to say at present, the most beautiful. Certain people will think that such caution was necessary, just as it was perhaps necessary to accustom the public to the *Pastoral Symphony,* to acclimatize them gradually, before offering them the *Symphony with Chorus.* If it was really a good thing to delay for a while and to limit the public's first curiosity to *Poor Folk, House of the Dead,* and *Crime and Punishment,* to-day it is high time for readers to tackle the great works: *The Idiot, The Possessed,* and above all *The Brothers Karamazov.*

This novel is Dostoevsky's last work. It was to have been the first of a series. Dostoevsky was then fifty-nine. He wrote:

"You can't imagine how many times I have examined myself only to discover that I have not expressed literally the twentieth part of what was in my mind, and what could, perhaps, have been expressed! My salvation lies in the sure hope that one day God may grant me such strength and inspiration that I shall find perfect self-expression and be able to make plain all that I carry in my heart and imagination."

Dostoevsky was one of those rare geniuses who proceed from work to work in a kind of constant progression until death brings them to an abrupt halt. No sign of decline in that ardent old age, any more than in Rembrandt's or Beethoven's, with whom I like to compare him; a constant and intense augmentation of mental power.

Never indulgent towards himself, always dissatisfied, demanding even the impossible, yet fully conscious of his own value—before beginning *The Brothers Karamazov* he had felt a strange prophetic joy. Here at last was a subject cut to his measure, to the measure of his genius.

"I have seldom," he wrote, "had the good fortune to have something so new, so complete, so original to say."

This was the book on Tolstoy's bedside table when he died.

Its first translator, appalled by its length, gave us only a mutilated version of this incomparable work. With the excuse of over-all unity whole chapters were amputated here and there, enough to form an additional volume which was published under the title *The Precocious,* and as a further precaution, which succeeded in misleading the reader completely, the name Karamazov was changed to Chestomazov. But this mutilated translation was in fact very good as far as it went, and I still prefer it to the one that was given to us later. Considering the period at which it appeared, some people will think that the public at the time was not yet ready for a masterpiece of such prodigality. Therefore, the only objection I shall make is that the public was not told at once that the translation was incomplete.

Four years ago the new translation by Messrs. Bienstock and Nau appeared. It had this great advantage that it presented the general plan of the work in a more concise volume; I mean that it restored to their proper place the parts that the first translation had omitted. But by a systematic condensation, I almost said congelation, they stripped the dialogues of their pathetic stammerings and flounderings, they skipped a third of the sentences, often whole paragraphs, and the most significant ones. The result is clear, abrupt, without shading, like a Rembrandt engraving, or rather a line drawing, as compared with the depth of the paintings. Yet what virtue Dostoevsky's book must have to remain admirable in spite of all these degradations! A book that could patiently await its time as Stendhal's books patiently awaited theirs; a book whose time has at last arrived.

In Germany translations of Dostoevsky follow one upon the other, each an improvement in scrupulous accuracy and vivacity on the one before. Even England, always slower and more refractory, has taken pains not to be left behind. In New Age of the twenty-third of last March, Arnold Bennett, announcing Mrs. Constance Garnett's translation, expresses the hope that English novelists and short-story writers may learn something from "the most powerful works of imagination ever written," and speaking more specifically of The Brothers Karamazov: "Here," he says, "passion reaches the very height of its power. This book introduces a dozen absolutely colossal figures."

Who can say whether these "colossal figures" did not point more directly to us than to anyone else, even in Russia, or whether before our own time their voice would have seemed so urgent? Ivan, Dmitri, Alyosha, the three brothers, so different and so akin, followed everywhere and constantly troubled by their pitiful shadow, Smerdiakov, their servant and half-brother. The intellectual Ivan, the passionate Dmitri, Alyosha the mystic, seem to divide between them the moral world which their old father shamefully abandons—and I know that they are already exerting an unrestricted influence on many young men. Their voice no longer seems strange to us, or rather, I should say that it is in ourselves we hear them speaking. Yet at the same time no obtrusive symbolism in the construction of the work. We know that the initial pretext for this novel was an ordinary newspaper story, a mystifying "case," which this subtle psychologist set himself to elucidate. Nothing could be more constantly alive than these significant figures; not for an instant do they escape their importunate reality.

To-day, now that they are going on the stage (and of all the creations of the imagination or of all history's heroes, there are none that have a better right to a stage career), to-day the question is whether in the actors' studied intonations we will recognize their disconcerting voices.

The question is whether the author of the adaptation will be able to present without too much distortion the events essential to the plot in which these characters are brought together. I believe him to be extremely intelligent and skilful; I am sure he understands that to meet the demands of the theatre it is not enough just to cut, as is usually done, and present baldly the novel's most dramatic episodes, but that it is necessary to go back to the origin of the work, to abridge it and to arrange its elements with a view to a different perspective.

And finally the question is whether the people in the audience who have not already penetrated the work will be willing to give to these "colossal figures" all the attention necessary. At least, they are not likely to have that "extraordinary presumption, that phenomenal ignorance," which

Dostoevsky deplored in the Russian intellectuals. But his hope was, "to turn them from their negative attitude, or at least to make them stop and think, to make them doubt."

And what I have just said has no other aim.

APPENDIX

I

"AND now I will tell two anecdotes to wind up my account of the '*idea*,' that it may not hinder my story again.

"In July, two months before I came to St. Petersburg, when my time was all my own, Marie Ivanovna asked me to go to see an old maiden lady who was staying in the Troitsky suburb to take her a message of no interest for my story. Returning the same day, I noticed in the railway carriage an unattractive-looking young man, not very poorly though grubbily dressed, with a pimply face and a muddy dark complexion. He distinguished himself by getting out at every station, big and little, to have a drink. Towards the end of the journey he was surrounded by a merry throng of very low companions. One merchant, also a little drunk, was particularly delighted at the young man's power of drinking incessantly without becoming drunk. Another person, who was awfully pleased with him, was a very stupid fellow who talked a great deal. He was wearing European dress and smelt most unsavoury—he was a footman, as I found out afterwards: this fellow got quite friendly with the young man who was drinking and, every time the train stopped, roused him with the invitation, 'It's time for a drop of vodka,' and they got out with their arms round each other. The young man who drank scarcely said a word, but yet more and more companions joined him. He only listened to their chatter, grinning incessantly with a drivelling snigger, and only from time to time, always unexpectedly, brought out a sound something like 'Ture-lure-loo!' while he put his finger up to his nose in a very comical way. This diverted the merchant, and the footman and all of them, and they burst into a very loud and free and easy laughter. It is sometimes impossible to understand why people laugh. I joined them, too, and I don't know why, the young man attracted me too, perhaps by his very open disregard for the generally accepted conventions and proprieties. I didn't see, in fact, that he was simply a fool. Anyway, I got on to friendly terms with him at once, and as I got out of the train, I learnt from him that he would be in the Tverskoy Boulevard between eight and nine. It appeared that he had been a student. I went to the boulevard, and this was the diversion he taught me. We walked together up and down the boulevards, and, a little later, as soon as we noticed a respectable woman walking along the street, if there were no one else near, we fastened upon her. Without uttering a word we walked one on each side of her, and with an air of perfect composure, as though we didn't see her, began to carry on a most unseemly conversation. We called things by their names, preserving unruffled countenances as though it were the natural thing to do; we entered into such subtleties in our description of all sorts of filth and obscenity as the nastiest mind of the lewdest debauchee could scarcely have conceived. (I had, of course, acquired all this knowledge at the boarding school, before I went to the Grammar School, though I knew only words, nothing of the reality.) The woman was dreadfully frightened, and made haste to try and get away, but we quickened our pace too, and went on in the same way. Our victim, of course, could do nothing; it would be no use to cry out, there were no spectators; besides, it would be a strange thing to complain of. I repeated this diversion for eight days. I can't think how I can have liked doing it; although, indeed, I didn't like doing it—I simply did it. At first I thought it original, as something outside everyday conventions and conditions, besides, I couldn't endure women. I once told the student that in his *Confessions* Jean Jacques Rosseau describes how, as a youth, he used to behave indecently to women. The student responded with his 'Ture-lure-lool' I noticed that he was extraordinarily ignorant, and that his interests were astonishingly limited. There was no trace of any latent idea such as I hoped to find in him. Instead of originality, I found nothing but a wearisome monotony. I disliked him more and more. The end came quite unexpectedly. One night when it was quite dark, we persecuted a girl who was quickly and timidly walking along the boulevard. She was very young, perhaps sixteen, or even less, very tidily and modestly dressed, possibly a working girl hurrying home to an old widowed mother with other children; there is no need to be sentimental though. The girl listened for some time, and hurried fast as she could with her head bowed and her veil drawn over her face, frightened and trembling. But suddenly she stood still, threw back her veil, showing, as far as I remember, a thin but pretty face, and cried with flashing eyes:

" 'Oh, what scoundrels you are!'

"She may have been on the verge of tears, but something different happened. Lifting her thin little hand, she gave the student a slap in the face which could not have been more dexterously delivered. It did come with a smack! He would have rushed at her, swearing, but I held him back, and the girl had time to run away. We began quarrelling at once. I told him all that I had been saving up against him in those days. I told him that he was the paltriest commonplace fool without the trace of an idea. He swore at me. . . . (I had once explained to him that I was illegitimate.) Then we spat at each other, and I've never seen him since. I felt frightfully vexed with myself that evening, but not so much the next day, and by the day after that had quite forgotten it. And though I sometimes thought of the girl again, it was only casually, for a moment. It was only after I'd been a fortnight in Petersburg I suddenly recalled the whole scene. I remembered it, and I was suddenly so ashamed that tears of shame literally ran down my cheeks. I was wretched the whole evening, and all that night, and I am rather miserable about it now. I could not understand at first how I could have sunk to such a depth of degradation, and still less how I could have forgotten it without feeling shame or remorse. It is only now that I understand what was at the root of it; it was all due to my '*idea*'. . . . The '*idea*' comforted me in disgrace and insignificance. But all the nasty things I did took refuge, as it were, under the '*idea*'. It, so to speak, smoothed over everything, but it also put a mist before my eyes, and such a misty understanding of things and events may, of course, be a great hindrance to the '*idea*' itself, to say nothing of other things.

"Now for another anecdote.

"On the 1st of April last year, Marie Ivanovna was keeping her name day; some visitors, though only a few, came for the evening. Suddenly Agrafena rushed in, out of breath, announcing that a baby was crying in the passage before the kitchen, and that she didn't know what to do. We were all excited at the news. We went out and saw a bark basket, and in the basket a three- or four-week-old child, crying. I picked up the basket and took it into the kitchen. Then I immediately found a folded note:

" 'Gracious benefactors, show kind charity to the girl christened Arina, and we will join with her to send our tears to the Heavenly Throne for you for ever, and congratulate you on your name day. " 'Persons unknown to you.'

"Then Nikolay Semyonovitch, for whom I have such a respect, greatly disappointed me. He drew a very long face, and decided to send the child at once to the Foundling Home. I felt very sad. They lived frugally and had no children and Nikolay Semyonovitch was always glad of it. I carefully took the little Arina out of the basket and held her up under the arms. The basket had that sour, pungent odour characteristic of a small child which has not been washed for a long time. I opposed Nikolay Semyonovitch and suddenly announced that I would keep the child at my expense. In spite of his gentleness he protested with some severity, and, though he ended by joking, he adhered to his intention in regard to the foundling. I got my way, however. In the same block of buildings, but in a different wing, lived a very poor carpenter, an elderly man, given to drink, but his wife, a very healthy and still youngish woman, had only just lost a baby, and what is more, the only child she had had in eight years of marriage, also a girl, and by a strange piece of luck also called Arina. I call it good luck, because while we were arguing in the kitchen, the woman, hearing of what had happened, ran in to look at the child, and when she learned that it was called Arina, she was greatly touched. She still had milk, and unfastening her dress, she put the baby to her breast. I began persuading her to take the child home with her, saying I would pay for it every month. She was afraid her husband would not allow it, but she took it for the night. Next morning, her husband consented to her keeping it for eight roubles a month, and I immediately paid him for the first month in advance. He at once spent the money on drink. Nikolay Semyonovitch, still with a strange smile, agreed to guarantee that the money would be paid regularly every month. I would have given my sixty roubles into Nikolay Semyonovitch's keeping as security, but he did not take it. He knew, however, that I had the money, and trusted me. Our momentary quarrel was smoothed over by this delicacy on his part. Marie Ivanovna said nothing, but wondered at my undertaking such a responsibility. I particularly appreciated their delicacy in refraining from the slightest jest at my expense, but on the contrary, taking the matter with proper seriousness. I used to run over to the carpenter's wife three times a day, and at the end of the week I slipped an extra three roubles into her hand without her husband's knowledge. For another three I bought a little quilt and swaddling clothes. But ten days later little Arina fell ill. I called in a doctor at once, he wrote a prescription, and we were up all night tormenting the mite with horrid medicine. Next day he declared that he had been sent for too late, and answered my entreaties—which I fancy were more like reproaches—by saying with majestic evasiveness: 'I am not God.' The baby's little tongue and lips and whole mouth were covered with a minute white rash and towards evening she died, gazing at me with her big black eyes as though she understood already. I don't know why I never thought to take a photograph of the dead baby. But will it be believed that I cried that evening, and, in fact, I howled as I had never let myself do before, and Marie Ivanovna had to try to comfort me, again without the least mockery either on her part or on Nikolay Semyonovitch's. The carpenter made a little coffin, and Marie Ivanovna finished it with a frill and a pretty little pillow, while I brought flowers and strewed them on the baby. So they carried away my poor little blossom, whom it will hardly be believed I can't forget even now. A little afterwards, however, this sudden adventure made me reflect seriously. Little Arina had not cost me much, of course, the coffin, the burial, the doctor, the flowers, and the payment of the carpenter's wife came altogether to thirty roubles. As I was going to Petersburg I made up this sum from forty roubles sent to me by Versilov, for the journey and from the sale of various articles before my departure, so that my capital remained intact. But I thought: 'If I am going to be turned aside like this, I shan't get far.' The affair with the student showed that the '*idea*' might absorb me till it blurred my impressions and drew me away from the realities of life. The incident with little Arina proved, on the contrary, that no '*idea*' was strong enough to absorb me, at least so completely that I should not stop short in the face of an overwhelming fact and sacrifice to it at once all that I had done for the '*idea*' by years of labour. Both conclusions were nevertheless true."[1]

II

" 'In what way can I be of use to you, honoured prince, since anyway you . . . called me just now,' he said at last after a brief silence.

A Raw Youth, pp. 88–93.

" 'Why, I asked you about the general,' Myshkin, who had been musing for a moment, answered hurriedly, 'and . . . in regard to that theft you told me about.'

" 'In regard to what?'

" 'Why, as though you don't understand me now! Oh dear, Lukyan Timofeyitch, you're always acting a part! The money, the money, the four hundred roubles you lost, that day in your pocket-book, and about which you came to tell me in the morning, as you were setting off for Petersburg. Do you understand at last?'

" 'Ah, you're talking about that four hundred roubles!' drawled Lebedyev, as though he had only just guessed. 'I thank you, prince, for your sincere sympathy: it is too flattering for me, but . . . I found them some time since.'

" 'Found them? Ah, thank God!'

" 'That exclamation is most generous on your part, for four hundred roubles is no small matter for a poor man who lives by his hard work, with a large family of motherless children . . .'

" 'But I didn't mean that! Of course, I am glad you found the money,' Myshkin corrected himself quickly, 'but how did you find it?'

" 'Very simply. I found it under the chair on which my coat had been hung, so that the pocket-book must have slipped out of the pocket on to the floor!'

" 'Under the chair? It's impossible! Why, you told me yourself you had hunted in every corner. How was it you came to overlook the most obvious place?'

" 'I should think I did look! I remember only too well how I looked! I crawled on all fours, felt the place with my hands, moving back the chairs because I couldn't trust my own eyes: I saw there was nothing there, for the place was as smooth and empty as my hands, and yet I went on fumbling. You always see that weakness in anyone who is very anxious to find anything, when anything serious and important has been lost. A man sees there's nothing there, the place is empty, and yet he peeps into it a dozen times.'

" 'Yes, I dare say; only, how was it seen? . . . I still don't understand,' muttered Myshkin, disconcerted. 'You told me before it wasn't there, and you had looked in that place, and then it suddenly turned up!'

" 'And then it suddenly turned up.'

"Myshkin looked strangely at Lebedyev. 'And the general?' he asked suddenly. 'What about the general? . . .' Lebedyev seemed at a loss again.

" 'Oh dear! I ask you what did the general say when you found the pocket-book under the chair? You looked for it together, you know.'

" 'We did look together before. But that time, I confess, I held my tongue, and preferred not to tell him that the pocket-book had been found by me and alone.'

" 'But . . . why? And the money—was it all there?'

" 'I opened the pocket-book. The money was untouched, every rouble of it.'

" 'You might have come to tell me,' Myshkin observed thoughtfully.

" 'I was afraid to disturb you, prince, in your personal and, so to say, absorbing interests, and besides, I made as though I had found nothing. I opened the pocket-book and looked at it, then I shut it and put it back under the chair.'

" 'But what for?'

" 'Oh, n-othing, from curiosity,' chuckled Lebedyev, rubbing his hands.

" 'Then it has been lying there since the day before yesterday?'

" 'Oh, no; it only lay there for a day and a night. You see it was partly that I wanted the general to find it. For since I found it, why should not the general notice the object, which lay conspicuous under the chair, so to speak, catching the eye.

" 'I lifted that chair several times and put it so that the pocket-book was completely in view, but the general simply didn't notice it, and so it went on for twenty-four hours. He seems to be extraordinarily unobservant now, and there's no making him out. He talks, tells stories, laughs, chuckles, and then flies into a violent temper with me. I don't know why. At last, as we were going out of the room, I left the door open on purpose; he hesitated, would have said something, most likely he was uneasy about the pocket-book with such a sum of money in it, but suddenly he flew into an awful rage and said nothing. Before we had gone two steps in the street, he left me and walked away in the other direction. We only met in the evening in the tavern.'

" 'But in the end you did take the pocket-book from under the chair?'

" 'No, it vanished from under the chair that same night.'

" 'Then where is it now?'

" 'Oh, here,' cried Lebedyev, laughing suddenly, drawing himself up to his full height and looking amiably at Myshkin. 'It suddenly turned up here, in the lappet of my coat. Here; won't you look, feel?'

"The left lappet of the coat had indeed been formed into something like a bag in front, in the most conspicuous place, and it was clear at once to the touch that there was a leather pocket-book there that had fallen down from a torn pocket.

" 'I took it out and looked. The money's all there. I dropped it in again, and so I've been walking about since yesterday morning. I carry it in my coat and it knocks against my legs.'

" 'And you take no notice of it?'

" 'And I take no notice of it. He-he! And would you believe it, honoured prince, though the subject is not worthy of so much notice on your part, my pockets were always perfectly good, and then a hole like that, all of a sudden, in one night! I began to look at it more curiously; it's as though someone had cut it with a penknife. Isn't it almost incredible?'

" 'And . . . the general?'

" 'He's been angry all day; both yesterday and to-day: fearfully ill-humoured. At one time he'd be beaming and hilarious till he began to pay me compliments, then he'd be sentimental to tears, then suddenly angry: so much so that I'd be frightened really, for I'm not a military man, after all. We were sitting yesterday in the tavern, and the lappet of my coat stood out as though by chance, in the most prominent way: a perfect mountain. He looked at it on the sly and was angry. He hasn't looked me straight in the face for a long time, unless he's very drunk or sentimental, but yester--day he gave me a look that made a shudder run down my spine. To-morrow, though, I mean to find the pocket-book, but I shall have an evening's fun with him before then.'

" 'Why are you tormenting him so?' cried Myshkin.

" 'I'm not tormenting him, prince, I'm not tormenting him,' Lebedyev replied with warmth. 'I sincerely love and—respect him; and now, whether you believe it or not, he's dearer to me than ever. I have come to appreciate him even more.'

" 'You love him and you torment him like this! Why, by the very act of putting the lost pocket-book where it could be seen under the chair and in your coat, by that alone he shows you that he doesn't want to deceive you, but with your open-hearted simplicity asks your forgiveness. Do you hear? He's asking your forgiveness. So he relies on the delicacy of your feelings, so he believes in your friendship for him. And yet you reduce to such humiliation a man like that—a most honest man!'

" 'Most honest, prince, most honest,' Lebedyev assented, with sparkling eyes. 'And you, most noble prince, are the only person capable of uttering that true word about him! For that, I am devoted to you, and ready to worship you, though I am rotten to the core with vices of all sorts! That's settled it! I will find the pocket-book now, at once, not to-morrow. Look, I will take it before your eyes; here it is. There's the money, untouched here. Take it, most noble prince, take care of it till to-morrow. To-morrow or next day I'll have it. And, you know, prince, it's evident that it must have been lying somewhere in my garden, hidden under some stone, the first night it was lost. What do you think?'

" 'Mind you don't tell him directly to his face that you've found the pocket-book. Let him simply see that there's nothing in the lappet of your coat, and he'll understand.'

" 'You think so? Wouldn't it be better to tell him I have found it, and to pretend I had not guessed about it till now?'

" 'N-no,' Myshkin pondered, 'n-no; it's too late for that now. That's more risky. You'd really better not speak of it. Be kind to him, but—don't show too much, and—and—you know. . . .'

" 'I know, prince, I know. That is, I know that I shan't do it properly, perhaps, for one needs to have a heart like yours to do it. Besides, he's irritable and prone to it himself, he has begun to treat me too superciliously sometimes of late. One minute he is whimpering and embracing me, and then he'll suddenly begin to snub me, and sneer at me contemptuously, and then I just show him the lappet on purpose. He-he! Good-bye, prince; for it's clear I'm keeping you and interrupting you in your most interesting feelings, so to say. . . .'

" 'But for goodness' sake, the same secrecy as before.'

" 'Treading softly, treading softly!'

"But, though the matter was settled, Myshkin remained almost more puzzled than before. He awaited with impatience his interview with the general next day."[1]

[1] *The Idiot*, pp. 490-4.

New Directions Paperbooks

Eugenio Montale, *Selected Poems*.† NDP193.
Vladimir Nabokov, *Nikolai Gogol*. NDP78.
Pablo Neruda, *Captain's Verses*.† NDP345.
New Directions 17. (Anthology) NDP103.
New Directions 18. (Anthology) NDP163.
New Directions 19. (Anthology) NDP214.
New Directions 20. (Anthology) NDP248.
New Directions 21. (Anthology) NDP277.
New Directions 22. (Anthology) NDP291.
New Directions 23. (Anthology) NDP315.
New Directions 24. (Anthology) NDP332.
New Directions 25. (Anthology). NDP339.
Charles Olson, *Selected Writings*. NDP231.
George Oppen, *The Materials*. NDP122.
  Of Being Numerous. NDP245.
  This In Which. NDP201.
Wilfred Owen, *Collected Poems*. NDP210.
Nicanor Parra, *Emergency Poems*.† NDP333.
  Poems and Antipoems.† NDP242.
Boris Pasternak, *Safe Conduct*. NDP77.
Kenneth Patchen, *Aflame and Afun of
  Walking Faces*. NDP292.
  Because It Is. NDP83.
  But Even So. NDP265.
  Collected Poems. NDP284.
  Doubleheader. NDP211.
  Hallelujah Anyway. NDP219.
  In Quest of Candlelighters. NDP334.
  The Journal of Albion Moonlight. NDP99.
  Memoirs of a Shy Pornographer. NDP205.
  Selected Poems. NDP160.
  Sleepers Awake. NDP286.
  Wonderings. NDP320.
Octavio Paz, *Configurations*.† NDP303.
  Plays for a New Theater. (Anth.) NDP216.
Ezra Pound, *ABC of Reading*. NDP89.
  Classic Noh Theatre of Japan. NDP79.
  The Confucian Odes. NDP81.
  Confucius. NDP285.
  Confucius to Cummings. (Anth) NDP126.
  Guide to Kulchur. NDP257.
  Literary Essays. NDP250.
  Love Poems of Ancient Egypt. Gift Edition.
    NDP178.
  Pound/Joyce. NDP296.
  Selected Cantos. NDP304.
  Selected Letters 1907-1941. NDP317.
  Selected Poems. NDP66.
  The Spirit of Romance. NDP266.
  Translations.† (Enlarged Edition) NDP145.
Omar Pound, *Arabic and Persian Poems*.
  NDP305.
James Purdy, *Children Is All*. NDP327.
Raymond Queneau, *The Bark Tree*. NDP314.
Carl Rakosi, *Amulet*. NDP234.
  Ere-Voice. NDP321.
John Crowe Ransom, *Beating the Bushes*.
  NDP324.
Raja Rao, *Kanthapura*. NDP224.
Herbert Read, *The Green Child*. NDP208.
Pierre Reverdy, *Selected Poems*.† NDP346.
Kenneth Rexroth, *Assays*. NDP113.
  An Autobiographical Novel. NDP281.
  Bird in the Bush. NDP80.
  Collected Longer Poems. NDP309.
  Collected Shorter Poems. NDP243.
  Love and the Turning Year. NDP308.
  100 Poems from the Chinese. NDP192.
  100 Poems from the Japanese.† NDP147.
Charles Reznikoff, *By the Waters of Manhattan*.
  NDP121.

Testimony: The United States 1885-1890.
  NDP200.
Arthur Rimbaud, *Illuminations*.† NDP56.
  Season in Hell & Drunken Boat.† NDP97.
Saikaku Ihara, *The Life of an Amorous
  Woman*. NDP270.
St. John of the Cross, *The Poems of St. John of
  the Cross*.† NDP341.
Jean-Paul Sartre, *Baudelaire*. NDP233.
  Nausea. NDP82.
  The Wall (Intimacy). NDP272.
Delmore Schwartz, *Selected Poems*. NDP241.
Stevie Smith, *Selected Poems*. NDP159.
Gary Snyder, *The Back Country*. NDP249.
  Earth House Hold. NDP267.
  Regarding Wave. NDP306.
Enid Starkie, *Arthur Rimbaud*. NDP254.
Stendhal, *Lucien Leuwen*.
  Book I: *The Green Huntsman*. NDP107.
  Book II: *The Telegraph*. NDP108.
Jules Supervielle, *Selected Writings*.† NDP209.
Dylan Thomas, *Adventures in the Skin Trade*.
  NDP183.
  A Child's Christmas in Wales. Gift Edition.
    NDP181.
  Collected Poems 1934-1952. NDP316.
  The Doctor and the Devils. NDP297.
  Portrait of the Artist as a Young Dog.
    NDP51.
  Quite Early One Morning. NDP90.
  Under Milk Wood. NDP73.
Lionel Trilling, *E. M. Forster*. NDP189.
Martin Turnell, *Art of French Fiction*. NDP251.
  Baudelaire. NDP336.
Paul Valéry, *Selected Writings*.† NDP184.
Vernon Watkins, *Selected Poems*. NDP221.
Nathanael West, *Miss Lonelyhearts &
  Day of the Locust*. NDP125.
George F. Whicher, tr.,
  The Goliard Poets.† NDP206.
J. Willett, *Theatre of Bertolt Brecht*. NDP244.
Jonathan Williams, *An Ear in Bartram's Tree*.
  NDP335.
Tennessee Williams, *Hard Candy*. NDP225.
  Camino Real. NDP301.
  Dragon Country. NDP287.
  The Glass Menagerie. NDP218.
  In the Winter of Cities. NDP154.
  One Arm & Other Stories. NDP237.
  The Roman Spring of Mrs. Stone. NDP271.
  Small Craft Warnings. NDP348.
  27 Wagons Full of Cotton. NDP217.
William Carlos Williams,
  The William Carlos Williams Reader.
    NDP282.
  The Autobiography. NDP223.
  The Build-up. NDP259.
  The Farmers' Daughters. NDP106.
  Imaginations. NDP329.
  In the American Grain. NDP53.
  In the Money. NDP240.
  Many Loves. NDP191.
  Paterson. Complete. NDP152.
  Pictures from Brueghel. NDP118.
  The Selected Essays. NDP273.
  Selected Poems. NDP131.
  A Voyage to Pagany. NDP307.
  White Mule. NDP226.
Yvor Winters,
  Edwin Arlington Robinson. NDP326.
John D. Yohannan,
  Joseph and Potiphar's Wife. NDP262.

Complete descriptive catalog available free on request from
New Directions, 333 Sixth Avenue, New York 10014.   † Bilingual.